GO OUT AND MEET GOD

INTERNATIONAL THEOLOGICAL COMMENTARY

Fredrick Carlson Holmgren and George A. F. Knight
General Editors

Volumes now available

GO OUT AND MEET GOD

A Commentary on the Book of

Exodus

GODFREY ASHBY

WM. B. EERDMANS PUBLISHING CO., GRAND RAPIDS

THE HANDSEL PRESS LTD, EDINBURGH

© 1998 Wm. B. Eerdmans Publishing Company
Published jointly 1998 by Wm. B. Eerdmans Publishing Company,
255 Jefferson Ave. S.E., Grand Rapids, Michigan 49503
and by
The Handsel Press Limited
The Stables, Carberry, EH21 8PY, Scotland

03 02 01 00 99 98   7 6 5 4 3 2 1

Library of Congress Cataloging-in-Publication Data

Ashby, G. W. (Godfrey William)
Go out and meet God : a commentary on the
Book of Exodus / Godfrey Ashby.
p.   cm. — (International theological commentary)
Includes bibliographical references.
ISBN 0-8028-4332-8 (pbk. : alk. paper)
1. Bible. O.T. Exodus — Commentaries. I. Title. II. Series.
BS1245.3.A84   1998
222′.1207 — dc21   97-25268
CIP

CONTENTS

CONTENTS

EDITORS' PREFACE

The Old Testament alive in the Church: this is the goal of the *International Theological Commentary*. Arising out of changing, unsettled times, this Scripture speaks with an authentic voice to our own troubled world. It witnesses to God's ongoing purpose and to God's caring presence in the universe without ignoring those experiences of life that cause one to question God's existence and love. This commentary series is written by front-rank scholars who treasure the life of faith.

Addressed to ministers and Christian educators, the *International Theological Commentary* moves beyond the usual critical-historical approach to the Bible and offers a *theological* interpretation of the Hebrew text. Thus, engaging larger textual units of the biblical writings, the authors of these volumes assist the reader in the appreciation of the theology underlying the text as well as its place in the thought of the Hebrew Scriptures. But more, since the Bible is the book of the believing community, its text has acquired ever more meaning through an ongoing interpretation. This growth of interpretation may be found both within the Bible itself and in the continuing scholarship of the Church.

Contributors to the *International Theological Commentary* are Christians — persons who affirm the witness of the New Testament concerning Jesus Christ. For Christians, the Bible is *one* Scripture containing the Old and New Testaments. For this reason, a commentary on the Old Testament may not ignore the second part of the canon, namely, the New Testament.

Since its beginning, the Church has recognized a special relationship between the two Testaments. But the precise character of this bond has been difficult to define. Thousands of books and articles have discussed the issue. The diversity of views represented in these publications makes us aware that the Church is not of one mind in expressing the "how" of this relationship. The authors of this commentary share a developing consensus that any serious explanation of the Old Testament's relationship to the New will uphold the integrity of the Old Testament. Even though Christianity is rooted in the soil of the Hebrew Scriptures, the biblical interpreter must take care lest he or she "christianize" these Scriptures.

Authors writing in this commentary will, no doubt, hold varied views concerning *how* the Old Testament relates to the New. No attempt has been made to dictate one viewpoint in this matter. With the whole Church, we are convinced that the relationship between the two Testaments is real and substantial. But we recognize also the diversity of opinions among Christian scholars when they attempt to articulate fully the nature of this relationship.

In addition to the Christian Church, there exists another people for whom the Old Testament is important, namely, the Jewish community. Both Jews and Christians claim the Hebrew Bible as Scripture. Jews believe that the basic teachings of this Scripture point toward, and are developed by, the Talmud, which assumed its present form about 500 CE. On the other hand, Christians hold that the Old Testament finds its fulfillment in the New Testament. The Hebrew Bible, therefore, belongs to both the Church and the Synagogue.

Recent studies have demonstrated how profoundly early Christianity reflects a Jewish character. This fact is not surprising because the Christian movement arose out of the context of first-century Judaism. Further, Jesus himself was Jewish, as were the first Christians. It is to be expected, therefore, that Jewish and Christian interpretations of the Hebrew Bible will reveal similarities *and* disparities. Such is the case. The authors of the *International Theological Commentary* will refer to the various Jewish traditions that they consider important for an appreciation of the Old Testament text. Such references will enrich our understanding of certain biblical passages and, as an extra gift, offer us insight into the relationship of Judaism to early Christianity.

An important second aspect of the present series is its *international* character. In the past, Western church leaders were considered to be *the* leaders of the Church — at least by those living in the West! The theology and biblical exegesis done by these scholars dominated the thinking of the Church. Most commentaries were produced in the Western world and reflected the lifestyle, needs, and thoughts of its civilization. But the Christian Church is a worldwide community. People who belong to this universal Church reflect differing thoughts, needs, and lifestyles.

Today the fastest growing churches in the world are to be found, not in the West, but in Africa, Indonesia, South America, Korea, Taiwan, and elsewhere. By the end of this century, Christians in these areas will outnumber those who live in the West. In our age, especially, a commentary on the Bible must transcend the parochialism of Western civilization and be sensitive to issues that are the special problems of persons who live outside of the "Christian" West, issues such as race relations, personal survival and fulfillment, liberation, revolution, famine, tyranny, disease, war, the poor, and religion and state. Inspired of God, the authors of the Old Testament knew what life is like on the edge of existence. They addressed themselves to everyday people who often faced more than everyday problems. Refusing to limit God to the "spiritual," they portrayed God as one who heard and knew the cries of people in pain (see Exod. 3:7-8). The contributors to the *International Theological Commentary* are persons who prize the writings of these biblical authors as a word of life to our world today. They read the Hebrew Scriptures in the twin contexts of ancient Israel and our modern day.

The scholars selected as contributors underscore the international aspect of the series. Representing very different geographical, ideological, and ecclesiastical backgrounds, they come from more than seventeen countries. Besides scholars from such traditional countries as England, Scotland, France, Italy, Switzerland, Canada, New Zealand, Australia, South Africa, and the United States, contributors from the following places are included: Israel, Indonesia, India, Thailand, Singapore, Taiwan, and countries of Eastern Europe. Such diversity makes for richness of thought. Christian scholars living in Buddhist, Muslim, or Socialist lands may be able to offer the World Church insights into the biblical message — insights to which the scholarship of the West could be blind.

The proclamation of the biblical message is the focal concern of the *International Theological Commentary*. Generally speaking, the authors of these commentaries value the historical-critical studies of past scholars, but they are convinced that these studies by themselves are not enough. The Bible is more than an object of critical study; it is the revelation of God. In the written Word, God has disclosed himself and his will to humankind. Our authors see themselves as servants of the Word which, when rightly received, brings *shalom* to both the individual and the community.

— GEORGE A. F. KNIGHT
— FREDRICK CARLSON HOLMGREN

AUTHOR'S PREFACE

The book of Exodus is often seen only as history. As such, it seems largely irrelevant to most of the modern Western world. The aim of this commentary is not to provide a technical and critical explanation of the text and its formation. This has been done much better in the various works listed in the bibliography. Rather, the aim is to show the crucial importance of the events described and their meaning for the Old Testament gospel and to explain why the Exodus event is central to the gospel of Jesus Christ. Furthermore, the relevance of Exodus to the liberation struggle throughout the third world (and especially in South Africa) needs to be explored in a commentary on this vital book.

I here express my gratitude to the writers of various commentaries and other works touching Exodus. I remain grateful to Ulrich Simon, who first inspired me with love for the Old Testament and its theology. I thank George Knight for his generous encouragement and pastoral care (not many editors actually visit their contributors). I also thank Fredrick Holmgren and Daniel Harlow for their considerate editing. My best thanks go to my former secretary, Carole Law, who did much of the typing, but above all to my wife Sally for her advice on expression and in setting up much of the text.

— GODFREY ASHBY

FOREWORD

I have sometimes wondered whether the affluent and the power-ful — those who are successful and to some extent therefore self-sufficient — find it difficult to make an opening for grace, for the initiative of God which ends up with a free, unearned and, indeed, unearnable gift. Is this partly what Jesus meant when He spoke about the difficulty likely to be experienced by the rich in entering heaven?

These musings are germane to dealing with a commentary on Exodus. I have been struck increasingly by the fact that the Bible seems to have been written for people in trouble who often felt helpless and powerless, suffering as they often were under op-pressive rule at a time when religious people could be persecuted for their faith. Is it a coincidence that the Bible was written, as it were, out of suffering to bring succor and comfort to those who are themselves victims? Can those who are strong and success-ful hear the Bible speaking as deep speaking to deep? I am sure they can since the redeemed clearly include many from this group. Perhaps we should say that it is very difficult for grace to find an entree with the powerful and for them to hear the Scriptures in quite the same way as the hungry, the poor, the oppressed, and the scum of the earth.

What I certainly know is that it was exhilarating in my public ministry to preach the biblical message to our people in their distress through the oppression and injustice of apartheid. It was as if it had all been written with them in mind. How frequently I was able in South Africa, but also in other parts of our African continent (and sometimes on other continents), to speak about the God who had encountered Moses at the burning bush — the one who heard the cry of an oppressed rabble of slaves, who saw their suffering, who knew and who would come down to deliver them. Those were words that resonated among our people at mass funerals after yet another massacre by the security forces of the apartheid state, or by hit squads, or by a sinister third force that fueled what was gleefully described as "black-on-black violence," as if white-on-black or black-on-white violence might have been more tolerable.

In the depths of gloom and despair, these words about the God who acts brought solace and encouragement until the great vindication came when South Africa threw off the shackles of racist domination, when our people crossed their Red Sea and set out on the wilderness journey of transformation from repression to freedom to enter their promised land of a nonracist, nonsexist democracy.

Bishop Ashby has set out to produce a commentary that deliberately does not deal at any length with the minutiae of literary and other critical issues but concentrates on what the Exodus meant to the Israelites in their day and what it should mean for us today. This does not mean he eschews scholarly discussion. What is quite remarkable is how lightly he carries his very considerable erudition and profound knowledge of much recent scholarship.

The commentary brings Exodus very much to life as having a continuing relevance for our daily living. For instance, Bishop Ashby has shown that the detailed legislation relating to the Israelite cultus is not a tiresome red herring but designed to demonstrate that all of life is religious. As someone once put it, only sin is secular. Dealing with the cultus and the ordinary business of living in one breath, as it were, is to demonstrate the interconnectedness of life for the Israelite, denying all the false dichotomies so much beloved especially by the Western person.

In this commentary, Bishop Ashby shows the book of Exodus to depict a God who forever takes the initiative on behalf of those who do not deserve it. It is to malign the Old Testament, and the Pentateuch in particular, to describe it as being legalistic in the pejorative sense and to reduce its religion to the correct performance of a plethora of laws to curry favor with a God not too inclined to accept the supplicant.

No, the commentary shows that God first delivers this rabble of undeserving, stiff-necked slaves, that grace goes inevitably and always before, and that the Law is given after the great act of deliverance, not so that the Israelites should impress God and thus earn their deliverance, but in order to express their profound gratitude for what God has already done. Hence the importance of the preamble to the Decalogue. God identifies himself as the gracious God who has already delivered them and thus shows he has already chosen them. On that basis do the "thou shalt's" and the "thou shalt not's" issue forth. It is all Eucharistic, all thanksgiving, all celebratory and joyous. The Law should not have been a heavy yoke. It was meant to structure the life of God's people, a life of ever saying thank you to God for what God had gratuitously done for them. The Sabbath law, for example, was meant to be a constant reminder of the joyousness of life as belonging utterly to God, a reminder that all we are and all we have is gift.

Godfrey Ashby has reminded us in a masterly commentary of this mysterious God who acts on our behalf, enlisting all of creation on our behalf and always being there. This Immanuel goes before as a pillar of fire and a cloud to lead his people from all kinds of bondage — political, economic, social, and spiritual — to the freedom, the glorious freedom of his kingdom of grace and glory.

— ARCHBISHOP DESMOND TUTU

INTRODUCTION

The Exodus will never be forgotten. It has an everlasting appeal, not only to the followers of the three great religions that look back to it. It still appeals to many who seek an answer to their own problem of oppression. In the Old Testament, the Exodus is the central event; it is history clothed in faith. For the Hebrews, God proved himself and revealed his true character. He selected a people, liberated them from oppression, and brought them to a certain place at a certain time.

In the Old Testament, the origins of the human race and the small beginnings of the Hebrew people lead up to the Exodus-Sinai event. All subsequent events, the teachings of the prophets, and the hopes for the future, flow from Exodus-Sinai, for it was here that God covenanted with the Hebrews. They accepted God and the liberation he offered.

In the New Testament, Jesus' lifework and teaching are built on Exodus-Sinai. He proclaimed liberation for every sort of captive and at the same time called his own people and the whole human race back to God. It is wrong to be selective in our interpretation of Exodus. We must not ignore the hardship of the desert and identify the freeing of the Hebrew slaves only with liberation from sin and fear. Nor must we ignore the liberation from sin and see only political or economic liberation.

The theme of the book of Exodus is quite clear. God enabled one small group of miserably oppressed people to escape from tyranny. He chose them for himself, he confronted them, and he revealed himself as the one true God. He showed them who and what he was. He showed them what they were like and sent them on their way to begin a new life.

1

There would be failure and success, problems and prospects, insecurity and achievement. God was explicit in his expectations of the people and offered them love, comfort, and encouragement. The book of Exodus is greater than its commentators. The faith of the Hebrews demonstrates that. Whatever Israel became, God made it so through the Exodus and through the meeting at Sinai.

The giving of the Law at Sinai was the beginning of the community, but the seeds of the community were sown with the choice of Moses, with his acceptance of his calling at the burning bush, and later with the crossing of the Red Sea. This community established its identity at Sinai with the receiving of the Ten Commandments. This group of drifting bedouin, who had been forced into slave labor by the Egyptians, became a people with a God-given purpose beyond their needs and expectations.

What is described in the book of Exodus was seen by the writers, and by succeeding generations of Hebrews, as history. This must not be ignored, however much the intricate details have been exposed to the findings of archaeology and biblical criticism. Whatever modern scholars may make of the book of Exodus, the Hebrews saw it as their history. We need to consider and understand this before we investigate the actual details, because Exodus proclaims God to be in control of all history. That is the faith of Israel. Some may wish to dispute it, but that is the basic theology it proclaims. The ancient world believed that most of the events surrounding human life, the seasons, birth, and death, were the acts of unseen spirits or gods. They knew too of the priests and the kings and the Pharaohs with their divine powers. We are mindful of market forces, political tensions, global warming, and grave issues of world health. Exodus brought the Hebrews face-to-face with something quite different, a God not tied to natural phenomena but who plotted the path of history by means of a series of specific events. The Hebrew tradition claims this most forcibly.

The book of Exodus represents a finished work. It is therefore based on hindsight and on the interpretation of what has already happened. It sets forth what Israel *believed* about its past. Behind the book there may well stand different strands and different traditions and different documentary sources. Nevertheless, these various historical events and traditions have been woven together into one theology, one faith-history.

Exodus is concerned exclusively with the Hebrews. Nevertheless, there is plenty of evidence in the Old Testament itself that the creation of the whole cosmos (however it was understood then) and the Exodus belonged together. The book of Genesis is witness to this. So are many other works, such as Psalm 136. Exodus is not meant to be read or heard in isolation. The same God who created *all* people grieves over their sin and plans to rescue them. The Exodus and the event at Mount Sinai is the act of a creator-God, a pilot project for the rescuing of all humankind and all things.

The word "myth" has various meanings and can easily lead to misunderstandings. Since it has become virtually a technical term in theology and in other disciplines, it must be used. Myth does not in this context indicate a fairy story or legend or propaganda; nor does it imply that there is no truth in the stories designated myth. In this commentary, myth indicates that traditional story forms are being employed to hand down archetypal and basic truths. Perhaps "truth embodied in a tale" gives some indication of the value of the myths in the Bible and particularly those of the creation. If we see the Exodus as history and the creation stories as myth, then we will be drawing a distinction that was not drawn at the time when the Old Testament was written. When remote history and myth are combined, as they are in the Old Testament, they are difficult to distinguish from each other. Both are subordinate to the faith of Israel. This is what the Old Testament scholar, Sigmund Mowinckel, meant by the "mythification of history."

If God acted at Exodus-Sinai, then Israel had everything to hope for. If only social and economic forces produced the Exodus, then Israel had nothing to hope for; she had only her memories of past glories. This is the interplay of myth and theology in Exodus.

In this commentary, not much attention will be given to the way the material was put or, rather, grew together. Literary criticism and theories about sources can be researched elsewhere. This commentary concentrates instead on the living tradition that produced the book called Exodus. It considers what it meant at that time and what it means to us now. The challenge of Exodus to the captive Hebrews, "Go out and meet God," is intended as a challenge for all humankind.

OPPRESSION
Exodus 1:1–2:25

What we call the Masoretic Text is the traditional Hebrew text of the Old Testament assembled over a long period of years from the second century CE onwards. This traditional text uses the first word or two of each of the first three books of the Pentateuch as the title for that book. The Hebrew title for this second book of the Bible is "(These are the) Names." However, a need was felt by the translators of the Septuagint, the principal Greek translation of the Hebrew Scriptures made from the third to second century BCE, for a more specific title. They therefore chose the word "Exodus," which means "Going out." Thus the escape from Egypt became, by implication, the dominant theme of the book. The journey out from slavery to a new life, rather than the actual act of liberation, receives the emphasis. The title could well have been, "The Freeing of the Slaves." Instead, "Going out (of Egypt)" is a wider title that looks forward to the crossing of the sea, the wandering in the desert, the arrival at Mount Sinai, and the making of the covenant. All of these events together make up one great "moment" in the Hebrew tradition. This one great event dominates the rest of the Old Testament.

The first and perhaps the most important question to be raised about the origins of the book of Exodus concerns the nature of ancient Near Eastern literature and traditions. In studying Exodus, we are not looking at twentieth-century literature, hot off the press, but at ancient traditions that were written down long after the events they describe. One need not assume that stories, myths, and tales of miracles are of an early date and that orderly ritual and legal codes are of a later date. That would be to apply our standards of sophistication to all the various kinds of literature of

5

every age. Likewise, the philosophical, theological, and sociological theories of our age should not be imposed on other times and civilizations. It used to be assumed that religion developed steadily from the worship of sacred objects, like trees and standing stones, towards a lofty monotheism. More recently it has been proposed that a chain of "peoples' revolutions" spread across the eastern Mediterranean world at the same period as the Exodus from Egypt, in the second millennium BCE. On this view, the Exodus was one link in a chain of revolts. Such theories are doubtless based on some historical evidence. Nevertheless, the Exodus story cannot be forced into such a pattern. Its message is far too deep for this sort of treatment.

What was finally written down in Exodus represents the creed of Israel. This is borne out by the rest of the Old Testament. There may well have been several accounts of the Exodus and the wilderness wanderings, possibly belonging to different areas of Israel. These may each have emphasized different events. Martin Noth posited five *traditions* rather than documentary sources (the Exodus, the Promises, the Wilderness, Sinai, and the Entry into Canaan). These traditions were certainly transmitted orally long before they were written down, especially in their final form. Some of these accounts may well have originated in liturgies or liturgical events in the Temple or at some other, older shrine.

Nevertheless, the result is a statement of faith which says, "This is what we believe about ourselves and our own accounts of our origins prove this to us." It is therefore almost impossible to disentangle earlier accounts from the final version and then be certain that the design that has emerged is true to what actually took place.

The authors, and most certainly the final author, were consummate theologians. Whether we accept it or not, the book of Exodus itself asserts that the Hebrews had one tradition from the earliest times. This was that the one God had chosen them and had rescued them from slavery and had brought them through various adventures to one decisive, blinding revelation of himself at the holy mountain. This belief shaped their traditions and literature as well as their self-understanding.

1:1-7   This introduction is narrated as history, people-history. There is no effective way open to us to prove or disprove it by the methods of historical research. There are no certain records of the people whose names are mentioned, or of their arrival in Egypt. There were many comings and goings at that period between Egypt and Canaan. Groups of people referred to as "Habiru" are mentioned in the Amarna letters and in other contemporary or even earlier sources. Sometimes these wanderers are described as invaders, sometimes as settlers. It seems likely that there could be a link between the Habiru of the second millennium BCE and the specific group of Hebrews of the Exodus. Indeed, Israel's faith was built upon their belief that Joseph was a historical figure, and that the narrative of the descent into Egypt deals with historical fact. The account states that the ancestors of the tribes of Israel arrived in Egypt and settled in the Delta region (in Goshen) and began to "fill the land." The lineal connection between Jacob's sons and the tribes for whom they became ancestors is fraught with problems. It is now commonly assumed that those who escaped from Egypt were not a homogeneous group of ethnic Hebrews, but a mixed bunch of refugees, and that they collected various other peoples on their way into Canaan (Exod. 12:38). This appears to threaten the neat clan system tracing its ancestry back to the sons of the patriarch Jacob. Instead, a picture begins to emerge of a furtive escape and additions of discontented people en route. This doubtless is the beginning of the theory of a general Near Eastern revolt triggered off or gathering up a local escape from Egypt. Yet all these historical uncertainties do not really threaten the narrative. Rather, they concentrate attention on Yahweh's concern, not for a specific ethnic group, later to become known as the Israelites and readily distinguishable from all other groups, but for an ill-defined and probably mixed group of human beings. These people were to be the first target for his love and redemptive activity. Indeed, the Hebrew Scriptures point out again and again, sometimes very harshly and crudely (Ezekiel 16) and sometimes more prosaically (Deuteronomy 4), that God's continuing choice of Israel does not depend on them or on their moral fitness or racial purity. It depends upon God's faithfulness, his enduring love, his *ḥesed* (see Psalm 136). As in many ancestral traditions, it is the living links, rather than the historical accuracies, that matter. The Exodus narrative emphasizes the living link between the one ancestor, Abraham, and those who underwent the Exodus experience and those who occupied the Promised Land. Whether or not they were lineal or legal descendants, the tradition and religious experience of Abraham goes through its subsequent and decisive stage in the experience of his descendants. The necessary sequel comes when Joseph brings them to Egypt and they survive there and are ready for the next stage in their discovery of their identity and destiny. The same words used in v. 7 of the Hebrews being fruitful and multiplying are elsewhere used of Adam (Gen. 1:28), Noah (Gen. 9:1, 7), Abraham (Gen. 17:2, 6, 8; 18:18; 22:17; 26:4, 28), Jacob (Gen. 27:3; 35:11; 48:4), and Joseph (Gen. 41:52; 49:22). A theological thrust of the Pentateuch is that God's blessing is successively given to humankind as a whole and then to Israel.

Verse 5 speaks of "seventy persons" arriving in Egypt. "Person" is the best translation available in English for the Hebrew word *nepeš*, which means a total personality. But this Hebrew word also has a corporate sense and often indicates a key person together with his descendants and dependents — his extended family. So the seventy persons included the women and children who formed that family, "to the third and the fourth generation" (see Exod. 20:5). This understanding of family structures stands closer to family relationships and groupings as they are understood in Africa, rather than to the nuclear family and the concentration on the individual typical of Europe and North America.

This is *history* as seen by people who were proud of their tradition and who looked backward from their own lifetime over the generations, often without written records. It is not history in the sense of documents and dates. The dates and the documents are helpful and often crucial, when they exist. By themselves, though, they do not give us *human* history. Tolstoy attempted to make this clear when he wrote *War and Peace*. He showed the human reality of Napoleon's irruption across Europe in the lives of the characters of his book. The historical veracity or accuracy of the characters pales beside the human accuracy of the sheer effect of the campaigns on human lives.

Rameses II (1290-1224 BCE) may be the best candidate for

the Pharaoh of the Exodus (see v. 11) but he is never identified as such in the text. It is significant that he is always identified by his title (Pharaoh = king) and not by his actual name, unlike the Pharaohs mentioned in 1 and 2 Kings. It is as if we are being told that a contest between the divinity of Pharaoh and that of the God of the Hebrews is about to take place. So the text mentions Pharaoh, any Pharaoh, rather than a specific ruler. The Hebrews are, in Egypt, oppressed by "Pharaoh," the most powerful force known in the world of that time. Over against Pharaoh and Egypt, their God ranges himself, power against power.

1:7-14   We have no record of the Egyptian side of the argument. Forced labor was commonly used in the ancient world. The Egyptians used labor gangs, including their own people, as task forces on their building projects. There are several accounts in Egyptian records of the period concerning escaping slaves. The escapes would took place from the city of Rameses into the Sinai peninsula and the Egyptian army would pursue the fugitives. Predictably they chose to flee at night.

These labor gangs seem to have been "task forces," rather than permanent slave-labor gangs, for they seem to have been disbanded when the projects were completed. The practice still continues into our own century, the classic example being that of the Gulag Archipelago of Stalin's regime as described in Solzhenitzyn's *A Day in the Life of Ivan Denisovich*.

The full implications of the plight of one such task force are sparingly but clearly set out in these verses. First, there is a change of regime, a new Pharaoh or, more likely, a new dynasty as a result of some sort of coup. As a result, a group of free-ranging bedouin settlers find themselves arbitrarily turned overnight into slave labor. The government shows no understanding whatsoever of their rights or previous history, and there is no appeal. This must have been a profound shock and trauma for those bedouin. They had not been slaves before, but herdsmen who owned their own animals and ran their own affairs. Now they are slaves, and so virtually the property of their masters.

Secondly, they now constitute a threat to the Egyptians, whereas previously they posed no threat and had even been invited to settle in Egypt. They had taken advantage of their welcome and of the conditions in North Egypt and had borne children "so that the land was filled with them." This last accusation (v. 7) is a palpable exaggeration, since they seem to have remained in the Goshen area (Exod. 9:26). The accusation conceals a real fear in the mind of Pharaoh that they might join with enemy invaders. Pharaoh then plays on the prejudices and fears of his people to justify his own racist attitudes (vv. 9-10).

Here we have one of the classic scenarios of racial conflict, and some of the classic arguments are used here. One form this has taken in our own times in South Africa is the "swart gevaar" (black threat) argument. Another form is the anti-Semitism that Hitler fostered in Nazi Germany. We could easily point to many other examples of race hatred on both a large and small scale.

Such dark motives and fears lead to oppression coupled with economic exploitation. This is brought out by the very strong language of verses 11-14: "taskmasters," "to oppress them with forced labor," "oppressed," "ruthless," "made their lives bitter with hard service." This is, of course, only the beginning. Doubtless, if there had been an accountable minister of labor in the Egyptian government of the time, he would have explained to the nation that brick making is not oppressive, that the laborers were being fed at government expense, and that they were not the only ones being so employed. In the Hebrew consciousness and tradition, though, there is the strong, emotional conviction that they were heartlessly betrayed, oppressed, and persecuted, and were totally at the mercy of their oppressors. It is this conviction of being oppressed, justified or not, that needed — and still needs — to be heard and answered. For the Hebrews, God was about to do just that, to hear and to answer.

Rameses and Pithom are generally accepted as historic sites, northern cities rebuilt by the Ramessid dynasty of Pharaohs. The most likely sites, Tel er-Retabeh and San el-Hajar, are situated well in the north of Egypt and lie close to the Delta. Their location makes the use of local labor a logical course of action.

1:15-22 There is a second and more sinister result of the "Hebrew Threat" perceived by the Egyptians: genocide. At first this takes the form of orders given to the Hebrew midwives to kill all their male babies at birth, the females presumably being spared for use as concubines by the Egyptians in the future. This is really a forlorn hope. As if any Hebrew midwives would calmly exterminate all the boy babies of their own tribe or group! Midwives to this day still guarantee the survival of many societies and communities in the third world. The midwives are actually named, and it is said of them that they "feared God." The contrast with Pharaoh, who is not named, is remarkable, especially if they are Egyptian midwives. Naturally, the women refuse to comply with the order and, when questioned about the continuing growth in the Hebrew male birthrate, give the age-old excuse that Hebrew women were quicker and tougher than the Egyptian ladies; they produced their children and hid them before the midwives could reach them. This is a variant of the South African legend that rural black women have babies one day and are back hoeing the mealies the next day. A similar report reached the Austrian government in Vienna in the late nineteenth century about peasant women in the province of the Bukovina. Such reports cheapen the traumas of childbirth, but in this instance they ironically provide a useful excuse. The Hebrew women are described as being *ḥāyyôt* (v. 19) — a word that occurs only here in the Hebrew Bible. Some scholars translate the word as "beasts" and therefore understand it as an insult to the Hebrew women; nevertheless, there are no other biblical examples of the word "beast" being used as an insult in the way it is commonly used in English. Others propose that the word means "life-giving" or "lively" and that the Hebrew mothers were determined to preserve life. There would thus be an intentional link with Gen. 3:20, where Eve's name is given an etymology to indicate that she is the "mother of all living." This would reflect the theology of the final author of the Pentateuch, who was not merely an editor. Such links need not be regarded as fanciful. After all, the Pentateuch in its final form was seen as a unit, not as a collection of separate books bound together to form an anthology.

The birthstool (v. 16), literally "a pair of stones," has usually been taken as a reference to the custom of a woman giving birth while kneeling or squatting on stones. However, the use of the dual in Hebrew (a pair of stones) makes better sense as a euphemism for the male sex organ. It is, in fact, far less of a euphemism than the English colloquial expression, "balls"! This certainly fits the context well, since the midwives would naturally be instructed to identify boy babies in this way. The midwives do not cooperate, but exercise "creative disobedience," as one commentator has put it. So the Pharaoh resorts to "the final solution." All male babies must be drowned in the Nile, possibly as an offering to the river god. Eventually, the Hebrews will be exterminated from Egypt. The females will then be absorbed into the local population and lost. Herod's small-scale massacre (Matt. 2:16) may have been seen as an echo of this. At any rate, this event has become the paradigm of similar events over the centuries. Fear and envy of one group of people, seen as interlopers by another group, lead to their being perceived as a threat to the resident owners of the territory. This perceived threat then leads to fear, resentment, discrimination, oppression, persecution, and eventually to extermination. The plan is averted by the action of the midwives and of Moses' mother and of Pharaoh's own daughter. Even Pharaoh is heard to command emphatically, and somewhat unnecessarily, that the *daughters,* as opposed to the sons, will live. It is perhaps significant that the males in the story of the Exodus are linked with oppression, slavery, and death, whereas the females are linked with compassion and the preservation of life.

2:1-10   The campaign of extermination misfires. The baby who, of all Hebrew babies, proved to be the greatest threat is miraculously preserved in the bosom of the Nile, the river in which he should have been drowned and thus been offered to the river god. This familiar story of a baby exposed to die — a foundling who becomes a great leader — occurs many times in ancient history and legend. Hercules and Romulus and Remus of Rome are examples, which could be matched from other cultures across the world. The nearest story to that of Moses is the Babylonian legend of Sargon of Akkad, who is also put into the river in a basket and adopted by the gods. The story of Moses' birth is told as sober history where no god, not even Yahweh, is mentioned. The story is woven into the Exodus event, where it indicates the outstanding destiny of Moses and is an ironic answer to the ultimate solution for the removal of the Hebrews. A helpless child will be God's instrument to deliver his people.

The tribe of Levi (v. 1), to which Moses belongs, presents a problem in origins. The tribal ancestor was cursed for his violent action in Genesis 34, yet his descendants later held a monopoly on the priestly office. Nevertheless, despite this apparent monopoly there are many examples throughout the historical books of sacrifices being offered by heads of families, kings, and other non-Levites. It has been assumed that as society in Israel became more stable, the performance of the liturgy was entrusted to a hereditary caste. This caste derived its authority from Moses, and especially from his brother Aaron. What happened to the original tribe of Levi can only be traced to the curse of the ancestor Levi (Gen. 48:5-7). The tribe, certainly according to the tradition associated with the Priestly source of the Pentateuch, eventually developed into a profession.

There is more to Moses' mother's perception of her son as "a fine baby" (v. 2) than may at first appear. Most mothers admire their babies, when most relatives and friends (especially the males) cannot see anything remarkable about them. This verse points to far more than Moses being a pretty and healthy baby. It is an echo of the creation story (Genesis 1), where, after each day of creation God pronounces that day's work as "good." So also this day's work is good for God and for the Hebrews. It is fitting for Moses' mother, as it was to be for Mary (Luke 1:31-33), that she makes this truly prophetic pronouncement. God will employ Moses to bring good from evil.

The Hebrew word translated "basket" is a general word for a chest or box, of any size; the same Hebrew word is used for Noah's ark. Both are safe containers, preserving their living contents from harm.

Pharaoh's daughter is anonymous, as is Pharaoh himself. Later writers obviously wanted to anchor the story to specific historical events. This process begins as early as the postbiblical book of *Jubilees,* where she is given the name Tharmuth. The original account is not so concerned with anchoring the story in historical names; the story itself is the anchor.

13

Seti I seems to be the most likely candidate for the Pharaoh whose death is recorded in verse 23. However, it is significant that his daughter, despite her race and family, takes her place as a preserver of life for God. The statement "She took him as her son" is probaby an adoption formula, of which there are similar examples in Ugaritic literature and Hammurabi's code.

The word used for the girl who watches Pharaoh's daughter finding the infant is the same as that used in the Hebrew text of Isa. 7:14 and denotes a young woman of marriageable age. Her mother becomes the child's wet nurse, appropriately enough, until the baby can be weaned and then handed over to her adopting parent. All three women have an essential role in Moses' birth and growth and therefore in the whole Exodus event. Their role is unthreatening and unthreatened. They ensure that the salvation event will take place. Together, the women outsmart the very ruler whose court was considered the pinnacle of wisdom in the ancient Near East. There is, in fact, a chain of such roles in the Bible, all the way from Sarah to Mary.

The explanation of Moses' name in verse 10 is not a serious piece of etymology but a pun. Hebrew writers used such plays on words not as jokes but in order to make valid theological points. According to the text "Moses" means "pulled out" of danger, rescued. The real etymology could also be significant. There were several Pharaohs with similar regnal names (Ahmose, Thutmose), and the second half of the name *(Mose)* means "born of . . ." coupled with the name of a god. A later Hebrew tradition, reflected in Acts 7:22, made much of Moses' education. This is not emphasized in Exodus, but the combination of Hebrew slave parents, an upbringing in the most sophisticated milieu available at that time, and subsequent marriage to the daughter of a free tribal chief — together this makes an impressive and a universalistic biography.

2:11-14   According to one commentator, "The present story reveals much of the character of Moses: his readiness to take the initiative in identifying himself with his people, his passionate sense of justice, his capacity for flaming anger, and his tendency on occasion to impetuous action" (J. P. Hyatt, *Exodus,* 66). These

verses, though, give another side to the seemingly heroic beginning of Moses' career. He certainly acts impetuously and
passionately in intervening on behalf of those he has now identified as his own people. His actions, however, are those of a
privileged and protected individual who suddenly realizes how
the other half lives. His actions are those of a raw and untried
champion of civil rights. He tackles the oppression of his newly
discovered people head on, by violent action, by taking the law
into his own hands. His motives are understandably misunderstood by another Hebrew and his crusading zeal changes to
furtive fear and an ignominious flight out of Egypt. This is perhaps
a truer interpretation of the intentions of the writer: to depict
Moses, not as a hero from cradle to grave, but as a meddling
unstable agitator to be transformed into a persevering leader. The
text nowhere states that Moses was acting, at that stage, under
Yahweh's orders. In fact, neither Moses nor the Hebrews have
any idea at this stage of who Yahweh is or of what he can do.
Moses begins his career as a failed political agitator, his bravado
turned into fear at the first show of opposition. This very human,
if not criminal, individual has much mileage to cover before he
is made fit to become Yahweh's agent in liberating his people.
Moses has acted and failed, and so he retreats. Yet at the time of
retreat, he is ready to learn the truth, ready for revelation from
Yahweh. Later he will return and begin the liberation struggle
again, only differently.

2:15-22   This pattern of action — retreat, revelation, return —
recurs in the lives of many religious heroes, such as Elijah, Paul,
Jesus, and Mohammed. So, in verses 15-22, Moses flees for succor
to his distant kinsmen, the Midianites. There is much debate as
to who the Midianites were and how they were related to the
Kenites and also concerning the extent of their influence upon
the faith of Moses. They belong to the background, while in the
foreground are the unique events of the burning bush and the
Sinai encounter, which completely dominate the "Midianite connection." If there ever was a previous Yahwist cult in the Sinai
desert, it certainly developed and flowered with the experiences
of the Hebrews.

In any case, the references are confusing. The Midianite tribal chief is given three different names (Reuel, Hobab, and Jethro), possibly indicating three related people. Nevertheless, whoever they were, these Midianites show true hospitality to an apparently vagrant Egyptian. He sorts out a dispute for them about communal use of a well (a vital matter in the desert) and is invited to share their food and hospitality and lifestyle ("break bread," v. 20). Interestingly enough, Moses' relationship with Midian begins with an incident of oppression. The women laboriously fill the troughs with water from the well for their stock only to be driven away by the lurking shepherds who use the water for their animals. This time Moses intervenes successfully on behalf of the exploited. He marries the chief's daughter, Zipporah. A son is born to them and given a punning and therefore significant name, Gershom, made to mean "Guest, stranger there."

2:23-25   Once again, strong words are used to describe the plight of the Hebrews in their cry for help: they "groaned under their slavery," "they cried out for help," and their cry comes up to God. Their cry goes *up,* because they are appealing to a *higher* power. These physical images used of human contact with the deity or even of the deity himself are often written off as primitive anthropomorphisms. This is unnecessary. First, the language reflects the ancient understanding of the earth as a flat plate punctuated by mountains and valleys, and covered over by a solid blue dome; above lived the Creator himself. So prayers and offerings naturally go up, while blessings and curses come down. Secondly, where relationships are being described, human terms must necessarily be used. The God of the Bible is personal, and personal verbs, pronouns, and expressions are naturally appropriate when speaking of him and of his actions. No apologies need be made for anthropomorphisms. The Hebrews cry out for help. Yahweh *hears* them. He *remembers* his covenant with the patriarchs, Abraham, Isaac, and Jacob. He *sees* the people of Israel. He *knows* them. All four of these Hebrew verbs express human actions and are *active* verbs expressing far more than a cerebral or intuitive process. When God hears anyone, he responds; when he sees, he makes a move; when he knows, he enters into a relationship with the person concerned. When he *remembers* his covenant, he acts.

The tradition and pattern of several historically interlinked covenants (with Noah, with Abraham, with Jacob), all culminating in the Sinai covenant, may well be the work of one tradition, the Priestly tradition. Here the covenant is extended backwards in time to Israel's physical ancestors even though their beliefs appear to have been forgotten during the oppression in Egypt. The Hebrew slaves, whether they were all Hebrews or not, had lost their identity in their anonymous slavery. They are now about to find a new and yet an old identity, and it is the identity, rather than the actual genealogical descent, that is important to them. The giving of identity and the revelation of God both happen together in the great event of Exodus-Sinai.

"I HAVE HEARD"
Exodus 3:1–6:1

The Old Testament usually takes notice of places where encounters with God happen. These encounters tend to be associated with mountains, solitary trees, wells, or other salient features of the landscape. Most cultures have traditions and stories associated with certain places. In each case, it is not the historical accuracy of the association or of the story that matters. It is the living tradition that takes at least a part of its strength from that particular place. Thus in Psalm 137 the exiled Hebrews in Babylon long, not just for home, but for Zion (the Temple complex in Jerusalem). A place associated with some special encounter of the past can be seen as a sinister place or as a safe place. An example of this in modern fiction is to be found in Tolkien's *Lord of the Rings*, where the travelers journey from one safe or sinister place to another (Rivendell, Moria, Lothlorien) and each place inspires both feelings of safety and of threat. Mount Sinai (referred to as Horeb in these verses) has been identified with various locations — Jebel Musa in the Sinai peninsula, another peak in the vicinity, a hill above Kadesh Barnea, and even a mountain in northwestern Arabia. It may have had previous associations with a deity. For the Hebrews it is marked out forever in their living tradition as the place where Yahweh revealed himself decisively, first to Moses alone and then later to all Israel.

Later still, Elijah returned to Mount Horeb in order to seek out the origins of Israel's faith and to revive his own vocation as renewer of that faith (1 Kings 19). In the same way, Luke 9:31 describes Jesus on the Mount of Transfiguration accompanied by Moses and Elijah. The three of them speak about Jesus' impending "exodus" to be accomplished at Jerusalem. This significant word

18

is concealed in English translations by their use of the word "departure." Reference to Jesus' "exodus" evokes both the Exodus led by Moses and Elijah's "exodus" in glory.

In Hebrew religion God reveals himself in particular places, times, and persons. So Moses, a special person, meets Yahweh totally unexpectedly at a special place and at a special time. A bush catches alight and is not scorched, shriveled, or charred. This is the initial sign.

In the Bible such events as the burning bush are usually called *signs,* not miracles. This is significant since it shows that the biblical authors did not view such phenomena as verifiable chemical or geological events but as *communications.* The purpose of the burning bush is not to demonstrate that bushes can burn without being incinerated, or even that the God of the Hebrews has the power to upset the ordinary processes, but that he is present and is about to speak with Moses. In any case, unusual fire or light frequently announces the presence of God, as in Elijah's chariot and Jesus' transfiguration. If we seek "natural" explanations, then it is indeed possible that this particular bush had naturally russet leaves, like the imidubi trees in Transkei, and that the setting or rising sun caught them — some form of petroleum explosion seems a little unlikely — but this is not the point. Yahweh chose this place, time, and happening to halt Moses, to introduce himself to him for the first time, and to call him decisively to a particular ministry. In the midst of his routine shepherding, the bush lights up at an unexpected time and place, and Moses is unexpectedly directed both to the God he scarcely knows and to the half-forgotten need of his people back in Egypt. The place becomes a shrine, and he removes his sandals. From this apparently insignificant beginning follow mighty events. Sinai is henceforward a holy place, so holy that Elijah returned here to gain the strength and assurance to bring Israel back to God. After him, nobody else is recorded as going there. The place had served its purpose.

The Old Testament is tantalizingly vague about dates. Even when kings' reigns are used for dating purposes, these are not as exact as we would like. One fairly obvious reason for this is that modern calendars were not then in use. People marked events by their seasons or by local events, such as the accessions of kings.

There is a more important reason, and that is that the biblical writers and their contemporaries were more concerned with the events themselves than with the exact chronology. It is now widely accepted that the distinction between the two Greek words, *kairos* and *chronos* has been overworked and that the semantic areas of the two words overlap. *Kairos* does not necessarily always mean "God's specially chosen occasion for intervention into history" as opposed to *chronos,* the simple date or time of day. This is to overload the two words and the distinction between them. Despite this, it is still true that it is the event rather than the date which is of paramount importance. Even if an exact date could have been given, the biblical writers were not concerned with protecting their accounts from the scrutiny of chroniclers of later ages. They simply put on record their conviction that at a certain time and place God acted.

3:1-6   Moses becomes a shepherd. In the ancient Near East, this was a responsible profession, not a job given to small boys. Kings were referred to as shepherds of their people, and God himself has that title (Isa. 40:11; 44:28, as has Jesus in John 12:14; Heb. 13:20; etc.)

"The angel of the Lord" (v. 4; Hebrew *malak,* messenger) is a device frequently used to indicate God himself, particularly when he goes into action and communicates himself in a special way. The expression "Name of the Lord" is used in a similar fashion. In the same passage, a writer will often proceed, as here, to refer to God simply as "the Lord."

Footwear (v. 5) was used for long journeys or for crossing difficult terrain, though people normally went about barefoot, as they still do in many warm countries. To remove the sandals is a sign of respect shown on entering someone else's home or territory. The Lord had marked out his presence and territory through the burning bush; Moses must respect this presence by taking off his sandals.

Yahweh identifies himself by his past relationship with the patriarchs and, unusually, by his relationship with Moses' own ancestry — "your father" (v. 6). This is his primary accreditation, the witness of past acts.

20

3:7-12   Having identified himself by fire and by his past relationship, Yahweh now takes up the present, the here and now.
By a series of dynamic verbs ("I have observed . . . I have heard
. . . I know . . . I have come down to deliver"), God forcefully
presents his plan of action to Moses. The promise for Israel is
outlined. The "good and broad land, a land flowing with milk
and honey," (v. 8) when offered to an oppressed and miserable
people, or to a nomadic people living from day to day, would
have been a blissful prospect. "Milk" indicates good grazing land
for cattle, and "honey" was the only natural sweetness available
at that time. This expression is often used in the Pentateuch but
is *not* the equivalent of *la dolce vita*. The biblical ideal, expressed
in Genesis 2, centers on a life that is livable and benevolent, not
a life of lazy affluence or greedy acquisition. It is a contradiction
of biblical doctrine for nations to provide an excess of goods and
perquisites for their populations (whether equally distributed or
not), while other nations have populations of starving people,
whether this be due to corruption, mismanagement, or climatic
hazards. The phrase "milk and honey" and what it signifies have
emphatically nothing to do with the "prosperity gospel" touted
in the Western nations and even adopted by some Christian
churches, who suppose that God blesses them by making them
affluent. This sort of theology is untrue to Scripture and simply
wrong.

The list of the inhabitants of Canaan (v. 8) should be compared
with the one in Genesis 10 (Noah's descendants). The lists are
not drawn up on ethnic lines. It is quite possible that the names
of the groups do not indicate racial groupings but classes or types
of people (e.g., peasants, town dwellers, etc.). But even if they
do indicate racial groupings, the picture remains a very confused
one. For example, the Hittites, who ruled a vast empire from
their capital in the mountains of Asia Minor (present-day Turkey)
were not a Semitic people. By contrast, the Amorites were certainly
a people of Semitic race like the Hebrews. Racial purity does not
appear to have been a political dogma in the ancient Near East.

Yahweh promises the land of Canaan to his people. Yahweh
has heard, and he will respond. That response will take the form
of land for the landless, a livable life for those whose lives are

presently intolerable. With life in the land will come the obligation to worship Yahweh. The Exodus story will not simply *describe* an act of liberation, but set forth a *theology* of liberation. Here we are shown that since God *is,* his promises must be believed and God himself worshipped.

Throughout the story of the Exodus, if not throughout the whole Bible, we are permitted to see God's dealings with people whose struggles are of tremendous importance to him and whose personalities he respects. Those who are brought closest to God retain their personalities, even in moments of closest contact.

Moses' protest of his inadequacy (v. 11) comes as a contrast to his earlier foray into revolutionary activity (2:12). He now needs the reassurance of a sign. But this time the sign given to him is not a physical, miraculous one like the burning bush, but an intangible promise, that he, Moses, will bring the Israelites to meet Yahweh at that very mountain. The sign, in fact, expresses the whole purpose of the escape from Egypt, which is to return to the mountain and *serve* Yahweh there. Biblical signs are revelations and are not necessarily physical miracles; they are not necessarily to be categorized as scientifically describable events, or even as miracles. (George Bernard Shaw was not so far from the truth when he had his cynical archbishop remark, in his play *St. Joan,* that a miracle is an act that creates faith.)

3:13-15   These verses contain key Hebrew theology, which has influenced Judeo-Christian thought and faith ever since. The language is simple and straightforward. Moses demands that this God identify himself, since he has promised so much and laid such a burden upon Moses' unwilling shoulders. Moses has to persuade the Hebrews back in Egypt to believe all that has been revealed to him and to trust him. Yet he will be a complete stranger to his own people, having been brought up as an Egyptian, not as a Hebrew, having had no share in their sufferings, and having spent the last few years far away from them living the life of a free, wandering nomad. When Moses asks God for the divine name he should relate to the Israelites, God answers him with the statement "I am who I am." This name is far from being a philosophical enigma or an early statement of the classic ontological argument. It rests at the heart of the Hebrew tradition of faith. Yahweh is himself, and this must be accepted in all dealings with him. Nobody will ever wield the power given by a name over him, or for him, or despite him. Moses can expect no further reassurance than that. He has to trust Yahweh, and that is all there is to it. Yahweh can only be known as he reveals himself.

The bush has burned but not scorched. Yahweh has spoken, and he has made promises. He has revealed such of his plans as he is prepared to reveal and has given a sign. He has also identified himself in the past of the Hebrews, in their genealogy (and genealogy for a nonliterate people is their history). He is the God of their patriarchs, Abraham, Isaac, and Jacob. It is a mistake to read these verses as a statement of technical monotheism when this would not have been the concern of the moment. They tell Moses what sort of God is commissioning him, and they sum up the living faith of Israel, faith in the God who acts.

The "I am" statement brings utter security, Yahweh's own security transmitted to Moses. It corresponds to the security the God of creation offered to the exiles in Isaiah 40–55 and to the "I am" sayings of Jesus in the Gospel of John. It also corresponds to Isa. 7:14, the "God-with-us" to come, and with Matt. 1:23 and Rev. 1:4, the "God-with-us" who has come.

The divine name *Yahweh,* technically called the tetragrammaton (Greek for "having four letters" — YHWH), is linked in this text etymologically with the Hebrew verb "to be." The original Hebrew texts were not "pointed" or vocalized; that is, only the consonants were written down. The reader had to put in and pronounce the appropriate vowels while reading. The pronunciation of the special name remains unknown and can only be guessed at, since it was never uttered. Instead, from early days the word *Adonai* ("Lord" in Hebrew) was uttered when the consonants YHWH were encountered. In more recent Jewish tradition, the word *(ha-) šem,* (the) "name," has been used. The spelling and pronunciation "Jehovah" is a medieval hybrid word invented by Christians who did not share the inhibitions of their Jewish contemporaries. They took the vowels of "Adonai" and adapted them to the consonants of the divine name.

The Greek translators of the Septuagint used the expression

egō eimi ho ōn, "I am the one who is" (or: "I am the existent one, the being"). Whether they intended it or not, this came to be seen as a philosophical statement, which had the effect of giving it credibility in the Greek intellectual world. However, the Hebrew language does not use tenses of the verb in the way that European languages do; present and future are indicated by the same form. Thus what God says to Moses is "I AM with you" or "It is I AM who is with you — that is my name." Yahweh is not a philosophical concept. He is the God of personal relationships, not an abstract, inscrutable Being.

3:16-22 The next task confronting Moses after he has convinced the Israelites is to go and see the Pharaoh. The escape from Egypt will not be a furtive stealing away or a violent breakout. Moses and the elders will approach Pharaoh with the authority of Yahweh and claim leave to trek out of Egypt on a proper journey. This is represented by the phrase "three days." Moses and Aaron propose to sacrifice to a god unknown to Pharaoh. Of course, the Pharaoh will refuse their request. The revelation of God's glory demands that Pharaoh be given the opportunity to refuse. Pharoah's refusal will provide the occasion to show the Hebrews and the Egyptians the sheer power and authority of Yahweh. There will be a mighty contest between the supposedly divine Pharaoh (and the deities thought to protect Egypt) and the real God who has taken the slaves of Egypt under his protection. The language of battles is used, for just as a victory by one army over another is followed by the looting of the valuables of the conquered, so will the Egyptians willingly despoil themselves of their jewelry. The jewelry itself will play an ambivalent role later in the narrative, since it will be used in the making of the golden calf (Exodus 32).

4:1-9 The question of credentials is now raised by Moses. Supposing the Hebrews in Egypt do not believe him when he, a man unknown to them, comes with promises of rescue from a god, also unknown to them? This time, visible and recognizable signs are given. Together the signs are not mere tricks to gain attention, but strategies in Yahweh's campaign.

In the first sign, Moses' shepherd's staff or crook becomes a snake and then, when grasped by the tail, becomes a staff again. This sign, possibly derived from snake-charming ritual, marks out Moses' credibility as Yahweh's minister and prophet. It also prefigures the healing and protective bronze serpent to be set up by Moses in the wilderness (Num. 21:6-9; cf. John 3:14). When this sign is later performed in Egypt (Exod. 7:8-13, by Aaron instead of Moses), the staff becomes a *tannîn* (serpent; dragon; sea monster) instead of a *nāḥāš* (snake) as in this incident. If the link with the episode in Numbers 21 is deliberate, this might explain why *nāḥāš* is used here and not in Exodus 7. In both these instances, a dangerous and sinister creature becomes a demonstration of God's power. Here the sign also indicates the danger facing Moses, since nobody with any experience of snakes would attempt to grasp one by the tail; it would immediately whip round and bite. A snake has to be grasped by the back of the head. Yet Moses is ordered to do the foolhardy act, since God will protect him when he interviews Pharaoh. This is the purpose of these signs. They are not in themselves miracles of healing or deliverance.

The second sign, the healing of leprosy, is not actually performed in Egypt, but it comes into play later as proof of Moses' authentic leadership in the power struggle with his own sister, Miriam (Numbers 12). The term "leprosy" covered a variety of serious skin diseases, including what is now medically defined by the term. It was seen as a direct affliction from God. For Moses' arm to become suddenly and horridly leprous would indeed have been a frighteningly authenticating sign.

The third sign, the turning of water into blood, will be performed in Egypt as the first of the plagues (Exod. 7:14-24). By it God, through Moses, will strike the divine, life-giving river Nile, and a divine blessing will become a sacrifice in blood. Life-giving water will become blood, bringing death to Egypt. Blood has one of two meanings in the Old Testament. It can mean murder and violence, or it can mean sacrifice. Here it indicates sacrifice. The river god becomes a sacrifice to the true God of the Hebrews.

4:10-17   Like Jeremiah after him (Jer. 1:6-9), Moses pleads his lack of talent for oratory. He is told firmly that this is Yahweh's problem and Yahweh's gift, not his. "Your brother Aaron, the Levite" will be spokesman. Aaron has a confusing role in the Exodus narrative, for he manufactures the golden calf at Sinai (Exodus 32), while Joshua appears as Moses' assistant and deputy afterwards (Exod. 33:1). In many religious traditions, gods are held to speak through the priests or oracles of their shrines. In Africa today, chiefs speak through their spokesmen, while either remaining silent themselves or speaking to them *sotto voce*. In any case, the role of the priest in Israel was not simply a liturgical one, but that of the interpreter of oracles and guardian and teacher of the tradition. Thus Aaron, traditionally the first and original priest of the Hebrews, is second to Moses, whose authority and leadership derive from God alone. God says "I will be with your mouth" (v. 12), a vivid expression of God's action by Moses.

4:18-20   Moses' return to Egypt contrasts with his flight from Egypt. He had left in fear and secrecy; now he returns with the blessing *(šālôm)* of his father-in-law, under orders from Yahweh. He returns in safety because those who sought his life have died. He returns with a plan of action to pursue, armed with his staff of office, which had been his shepherd's crook. This "rod of God" will later be used to strike the rock and provide water (Exod. 17:1-7; Num. 20:2-13).

4:21-23   Many people have been worried about Pharaoh's apparent lack of options. In the New Testament Paul writes about Pharaoh's hardness of heart (Rom. 9:14-16). Was Pharaoh denied a will of his own, and was there no possibility of his agreeing to Moses' demands and thereby doing God's will? The blunt truth is that the book of Exodus is not concerned with Pharaoh and his options but with Yahweh and his plan for the Hebrews. Further, since in Hebrew belief there can be no other basic causes for events apart from God (there is no god of evil who can frustrate the god of good), it is taken for granted that, if Pharaoh refuses to listen to Moses, it is God's plan that he should refuse. The prediction of Pharaoh's hardness of heart also shows a certain amount of political common sense. After all, what semidivine autocrat would listen to an outlawed demagogue who demanded the release of the state work force? The resistance of a tyrant is part of God's plan. In any case, Pharaoh's vacillations show his free will.

4:24-26 The circumcision of Moses' son by his wife Zipporah on their way back to Egypt is dismissed in many commentaries as an "obscure" incident. The origins of the story may indeed be obscure, and the exact details appear unclear. Nevertheless, it is unlikely that in such a work as the Pentateuch an incomprehensible and irrelevant piece of legend should be left unexplained and undigested. Five observations are pertinent here.

First, the event takes place on a journey and at a place with sinister associations. The similarities to Jacob's threatening encounter at a similar place — the drift, or ford, of Jabbok (Gen. 32:24-32) — cannot be purely accidental. In each case, Yahweh comes into close physical contact with his chosen person. In each case, the verb *nāga‛* ("touch") is used: Zipporah touches Moses with the foreskin; the wrestler touches Jacob's thigh. Both terms, "feet" in this story and "thigh" in the Jacob story, could be euphemisms for the genitals. The experience of Yahweh as adversary, threatening yet preserving, is a necessary part of the experience of God. *Fear,* including both awe and fright, does have its part in the human relationship with God, albeit not an exclusive part.

Second, circumcision is involved. This is an ancient rite of passage belonging to many cultures and marking one of three events in the life of a male (female circumcision is not mentioned in the Bible). It is performed shortly after birth, or at puberty, or before marriage. This last practice seems to be reflected in the account here and to have confused it, since for the Hebrews circumcision was a rite of birth (Gen. 17:10-12). However, the basic meaning of circumcision in the Hebrew tradition is acceptance to membership in the people of God. It was the sign of entrance into a corporate relationship with Yahweh, together with all the other people of Israel. The rite was not merely for hygienic purposes, nor was it racially distinctive, since various other peoples of the ancient Near East also practiced it. In the narrative, Moses has been brought up as an Egyptian, and he has been chosen to lead God's people out of Egypt. He therefore has to be adopted into Israel as a son to Yahweh. Hence, his son has to be circumcised.

Third, there is the pointed reference to the blood. Once again, sacrifice is indicated. Circumcision is one of the many types of sacrifice in which a small part of a person is cut off and presented as a token for the whole person. Circumcision is a form of human sacrifice, the offering of the firstborn male to the deity. This has great significance here. Moses' son's foreskin is the blood sacrifice demanded by Yahweh of the Hebrews, just as later in the narrative the whole crop of male firstborn will be the sacrifice demanded of the Egyptians. In both Old and New Testaments, blood frequently refers to sacrifice. Zipporah circumcises Gershom and, by touching Moses with the bloody foreskin, identifies Moses with that sacrifice. In this instance, there appears to be a motive of propitiation, since Yahweh appears to be angry and threatening. The operation is done with a flint to express, consciously or unconsciously, the antiquity and holiness of the rite or, quite simply, because a flint would have been sharper than a metal knife of the period. Zipporah's comment, "You are a bridegroom of blood" is not angrily sarcastic — "You are a fine bloody bridegroom!" — but a statement that Moses, by virtue of Gershom's blood, is well and truly within the covenant community that is about to be formed. Zipporah takes her place among the other life-giving and life-preserving women of Exodus. It is through her actions that Moses lives to lead Israel.

Fourth, some commentators have pointed out that Moses has been stubborn and has resisted God's call, just as the people of Israel will be later in the narrative of the wilderness wanderings. If the passage prefigures the wilderness wanderings, the intent may be to portray a God who is prepared to destroy the "son" he has liberated.

Fifth, God "tries to kill" but eventually does not kill. What sort of a murderous, yet hesitant, god is being shown here? There is no easy way out of this theological problem by substituting the words "tried to kill" with "fell seriously ill." The Hebrew words simply will not bear this interpretation. Rather, we have to accept that this is the language of threat, often used in the Old Testament.

There are many other examples. Abraham is ordered to sacrifice Isaac, and Isaac is reprieved (Gen. 22:11). Israel is frequently threatened with extinction by the prophets yet eventually escapes extinction after the Exile in Babylon. God's threats are neither tantrums nor concrete promises, but challenges to repentance, to negotiation, to mediation, and to reconciliation. In this instance, Moses has bent his will to that of Yahweh but has omitted the crucial rite of circumcision. Zipporah acts as mediator. As a "neutral" — since she is not a Hebrew and does not have to be circumcised herself — she persuades Yahweh to reprieve her husband. Another threat to the future of Israel is thus removed.

4:27-31 Moses, now totally conformed to the will of God, arrives in Egypt and presents his credentials to the elders. By the promised power of God, he is believed. They accept that God has heard their cry and they worship him. The word, even though mediated through both Moses and Aaron, is so effective that the signs are reenacted and the people believe. The liberation of Israel has now begun.

5:1-3 Moses seems to have had ready access to Pharaoh. This is not as improbable as it sounds, since Moses was brought up in the royal court, which at the Ramessid period was very near to the Delta and to the building operations. So Moses goes accompanied by his spokesman, which makes him more impressive than he would have been as a sole suppliant. Yahweh has laid down that Moses' first act must be to ask Pharaoh to let the Hebrews go. The reason given to him, to hold a feast to Yahweh in the desert, sounds like a pretext for escape. In fact, it is the fulfillment of the first sign given to Moses at the burning bush, to bring out the people to Sinai and serve God there. Moses is merely repeating what he has been told to say. He gives no promise of a return, and when met with Pharaoh's first refusal he adds to his request the purpose of the journey, namely, to sacrifice to the Lord. This is what "serving" the Lord must mean. It would normally bring with it the threat of reprisals from God if they defaulted. All this would have been readily understood by Pharaoh, since he was regarded as a divine figure himself and represented the gods of Egypt. He would have understood about demands for sacrifice and that epidemics and other disasters could be inflicted by gods who were not obeyed. But Pharaoh refuses. It will take more than threats from a god he does not know to make him let go of his labor force.

The feast is a "pilgrim feast" (Hebrew *ḥag*) involving a journey to a special place and days of celebrations held there. The sacrifice will be a *zebaḥ,* a type of sacrifice in which meat was roasted and eaten by the offerers and certain parts (e.g., the blood) were set aside for the deity. This may have been the origins of the Passover, a feast adapted from the customs of the Midianites, Moses' desert relations by marriage.

5:4-11 Predictably, the royal reaction is further oppression. It takes the form of harsh words and harsh treatment. Pharaoh assumes that the reason for this requested "holiday" is that the laborers are finding the work too hard (in fact, no mention has been made of hard work to him) and that they are lazy and idle. His reaction is to make the brick making harder and yet to demand the same amount per day. Mud bricks ("adobe" or "Kimberley" bricks) are often used in dry climates. Finely chopped straw binds the mud and makes for easier setting in the hot sun. Although mud bricks made without straw were at times used in ancient Egypt, in this case the order calls for straw, presumably delivered to the building site in carts. From now on the Hebrew laborers must first forage far and wide for their straw and also produce as many bricks as before. No wonder there was despair among the workers.

5:15-19 Pleas and complaints follow the new orders. This reveals the working of a "shop floor" system of Egyptian overseers set above Hebrew "boss boys" over the labor gangs. The advantage of being a boss boy would be, at the least, avoidance of manual labor, whereas the disadvantage would be that the weight of disapproval from above would land on them first. The brief interlude of hope brought by Moses now evaporates in the face of further misery. Life can only get worse with no possibility of improvement. Hopelessness is a prime element in oppression. As a result, the Hebrews take courage to reproach Pharaoh for wronging "your servants" and vent their frustration on Moses and Aaron (v. 19), who should have let well enough alone and not raised false hopes.

5:20–6:1   The spiral of blame comes into action, just as it did in Genesis 3, where under the Lord's accusation the man blames the woman, who in turn blames the snake. In this situation, under Pharaoh's attack, the Israelite boss boys blame Moses in strong language. Moses has made them stink in the nostrils of Pharaoh and has put a sword in the hand of the Egyptians to use against them. The spiral of blame is then completed by Moses himself, who reproaches Yahweh. Many of the Psalms also attack and reproach God, blaming him for some misery, problem, or disaster. This is not atheism or even rejection of God, but a baring of the emotions to the Almighty and the taking of the complaint to "head office," simply because the power to respond lies right there, with God himself. Psalm 22, used by Jesus on the Cross, offers a prime example. Wherever this happens, it does not bring swift retaliation from Yahweh upon those who have dared to complain, but an assurance that their complaint has been heard and a promise given of action. It also provides a means of working through real emotions. This is the biblical way of dealing with anger and frustration, rather than suppressing it. The result, in this instance, is the clear promise, "*Now* you shall see what I will do to Pharaoh."

LIBERATION
Exodus 6:2-27

Yahweh makes an emphatic promise to liberate an oppressed people. The liberation of the Hebrews from Egypt has become the paradigm of all liberation. It has been appropriated and adapted to many subsequent historical situations. To take but one example, the Afrikaner settlers traveled into the hinterland of what was to become South Africa to escape British rule in the Cape. These settlers saw themselves as taking part in another Exodus, with the British monarch as the contemporary Pharaoh. Their descendants were disconcerted to find that African preachers of the late twentieth century were calling for a fresh Exodus, with their own people in the role of the oppressed and with the architects of apartheid in the role of Pharaoh. In Latin America several contemporary liberation theologians, especially Gustavo Guttierrez and J. Severino Croatto, rely heavily on the Exodus as a scriptural basis for their theology. On the more popular level, Bob Marley's songs contain such lyrics as "Exodus, movement of the people" and "Then there's another brother, Moses, gone across the Red Sea. You've got to break oppression, rule equality, wipe away transgression, set the captives free." The Exodus is the starting point for God's "option for the poor."

Liberation theology must be taken seriously, though it need not be accepted completely and unconditionally. The avowed basis for liberation theology is Scripture, particularly the Exodus and the life and teachings of Jesus. Liberation theology has emerged out of life situations of need, in which the oppressed cry out for freedom from bondage, as the Hebrews did in Egypt. It is a pity that, even allowing for problems of translation from Spanish into English, the language of the Latin American theologians is highly convoluted and obviously not aimed at the poorest of the poor in Brazil. Liberation theology raises important questions of hermeneutics. How much should Scripture be recontextualized and applied to a present-day situation, separated from the original situation by many centuries? When does *exegesis* (reading meaning *out* of a text) turn into *eisegesis* (reading meaning *into* a text)? When can we legitimately apply a situation in Scripture to the present situation without placing our own ideas into the minds and motives of thinkers of many centuries ago? If we do this, we can easily make Scripture say something it was never intended to say. If, on the other hand, no attempt is made to apply Scripture to our situation, the Bible remains an interesting but irrelevant piece of history and literature.

Certainly the Exodus story begins with a cry for help arising from a situation of brutal oppression and threatened genocide. It is a cry of desperation. The situation could be described as a political and social crisis. In 1985, in South Africa, a group of theologians and pastors produced the Kairos document, *Challenge to the Church: A Theological Comment on the Political Crisis in South Africa*. In it they applied Exodus to the politics of the struggle, armed or nonviolent, against apartheid. Significantly, the Kairos document does give attention to the liberation of the oppress*or* as well as of the oppress*ee*. The document considers the ruling white cadre in South Africa just as much a prisoner of its own ideas and fears as the oppressed were of their plight. These concerns, for oppressor as well as for the oppressed, have been expressed in many other quarters, notably in the utterances of Archbishop Desmond Tutu. This stance contrasts with the absence, for the most part, of this double concern in Latin American writers and links up with the portrayal of Pharaoh as a person to be negotiated with *as a person* and not simply as an oppressor.

Was the Exodus primarily a sociopolitical act of liberation? Was it seen as such by the Hebrew tradition, which, after all, is the earliest interpretation we have of that event? Some scholars have seen the escape from Egypt as part of a widespread movement of unrest among city dwellers and tribesmen throughout the ancient Near East, directed against their rulers, the petty kings and priests. There is very little evidence for a movement of this sort, however many local disturbances there may have been. The theory looks suspiciously like the foisting of an international socialist movement onto a bygone age. In the Torah, the Exodus event is not primarily a political or social uprising. There is some truth in Croatto's assertion that "God did not begin saving in the spiritual order, not even from sin" (*Exodus*, 18). Yet the emphasis throughout the whole story is on Yahweh leading and inspiring a rather reluctant Moses and hesitant Aaron. What is more, the goal of the escape from Egypt is not that the Hebrews may yell, "We know we are free" but that they may shout, "We know our liberator, and he is Yahweh." The goal is that they commit themselves to him, make covenant with him, and serve him. It is the call of Yahweh to Israel to be his people that sets in motion the process of their liberation. Throughout, God takes the initiative because he is responsible for justice, even in Egypt. He must punish the oppressors in his own way. So, beyond taking their jewelry, the Hebrews inflict no damage on their oppressors. It is not they who take revenge on the Egyptians or on Pharaoh, but God, in his own way. They are not empowered to hold Nuremberg trials since it is Yahweh who is the judge, even in Egypt.

This is the thrust of the Hebrew tradition. There is no evidence that the Exodus was seen by the Hebrews to be *only* a revolutionary escape from Egypt. True, it is sometimes imperative to point out forcefully, as Latin American theologians do, that the Exodus was an act of justice and that by it God proved, right from the beginning, that he cared vitally and practically for justice in the lives of the poor and oppressed. But the Exodus was not simply an act of justice. It was first and foremost an *act of God*, concerned with his proper glory and revelation of himself as well as with the human need of a small, oppressed group of slaves. This is unmistakably shown from the beginning, when Moses acts violently in the interest of political justice (Exod. 2:12) and gets nowhere (other than into exile). Israel needed liberation in order to be free to meet and respond to the Liberator, Yahweh. Service to Yahweh is to replace slavery to Pharaoh. This must have been in Paul's mind when he kept on contrasting slavery to sin with service to God (Romans 6–8).

The Exodus is so dominant in the Old Testament that it is

necessary to see the aim of the trajectory set off by it across the Hebrew tradition. Far from leading to a series of heady revolutionary movements, each doomed to failure, the Exodus leads eventually to the Suffering Servant of Isaiah 40–55 and to the Cross of Jesus. Exodus-Sinai constitutes one event — the liberation of Israel that they might know their God and serve him.

6:3 Yahweh identifies himself not only as being the God of Abraham, Isaac, and Jacob but as having previously revealed himself to the patriarchs under a different name, *El Shaddai.* The word *El,* after a long history as a dominant god among many deities in various Semitic cultures (e.g., the city-state of Ugarit), appears in the Old Testament as the generic term for deity. The word is used throughout the Old Testament to refer to the God of the Hebrews and to gods worshipped by other peoples. The origin and meaning of the term *Shaddai* is less certain. In biblical usage, its primary sense has to do with *power.* Several scholars have associated the term with the mountains or, perhaps, the cosmic mountain of Canaanite mythology. Recently, the claim has been made that the people of Ugarit, living to the north of Canaan and at approximately the period of the Hebrew patriarchs, worshipped a god *Shēd,* whom they identified with their own child savior-god. This is probably the same god who was worshipped by the peoples of Phoenicia and of Palmyra under the name of *Shadrafa.* The same word, *shēd,* may have also become a general name for gods worshipped by other peoples, since it is used in that sense, in the plural, in Deut. 32:17 and Ps. 106:37. (The usual rendering "demons" in these two verses reflects a rather misguided effort to protect the monotheism of the Hebrews!) If this understanding of *Shaddai* is correct, then the author of Exodus combined two ancient names for dominant gods in Semitic culture. The power and prerogatives of *El* and *Shēd* are now taken over by Yahweh. He is the "All-powerful One." The name *El Shaddai* is translated *Pantokratōr,* "Almighty," in the Greek Septuagint and *Omnipotens* in the Latin Vulgate. In later Hebrew commentaries known as the Midrashim, *El Shaddai* is interpreted to mean "He who is enough."

Far from being an obscure piece of leftover polytheism, the name *El Shaddai* is a theological tour de force. The god known as *El* and the god known as *Shēd* by other Semites and known to the patriarchs as the All-Powerful One — that same God is now coming into action on behalf of their descendants. This underwrites and supports the promise of the land of Canaan, where the patriarchs had previously wandered around as mere sojourners. The covenant previously made with them (Genesis 15, 26, 35) will be fulfilled in their descendants and fulfilled fully, inasmuch as the land will now be theirs. The covenant made with the patriarch Abraham and repeated with his grandson Jacob concerned the future of the Hebrews. Its consummation at Sinai will involve their total and exclusive relationship with Yahweh. This is part of a covenant theology going back in the tradition to Abraham and even beyond him to Noah. This latter projection back to the covenant with Noah is most important, since it leaves the door wide open even within the Hebrew tradition itself for an all-embracing covenant between Yahweh and the whole of humanity. Noah is an ancestor of the whole human race, whereas Abraham is the ancestor of the Hebrews alone, even though he is repeatedly told that in him *all* nations will be blessed/bless themselves (Gen. 12:3).

6:6 Once again, a series of dynamic verbs emphasizes the program of liberation. "I will free you . . . deliver you . . . redeem you." This threefold formula is used 124 times in the Old Testament. The verb "redeem" (*gāʾal*) is frequently used to express God's action. Indeed, one of his titles is "Redeemer" (Isa. 41:14; 43:14; 48:17; etc.). Together these verbs indicate the sort of action Yahweh is expected to take, both in the present situation and always, as evidence of his very nature.

6:7 This verse looks forward to Sinai and shows clearly that the forthcoming covenant, far from being a political treaty or a "protection racket," is to be a *relationship*. The pronouns are strong and very emotive: *"I* will take *you* as *my* people. *I* will be *your* God." As in the creation stories (Genesis 1, 2), there is a third party in this relationship. This is the *land of Canaan*. God demonstrates his sovereignty over all the world by adopting Israel as a bridgehead and giving them a land to settle in and cultivate.

6:12   Moses is abashed and fearful of causing further hardship for the Hebrews. Once again he pleads his lack of oratorical skill. He says that he is "of uncircumcised lips" (RSV), meaning that his speech is not "free," so that he feels inadequate. "Uncircumcised" in this and in many other places has come to mean "incompetent," or, in this context, "halting" (NRSV).

6:14-27   Yahweh has chosen Israel as a whole, but he has also chosen individuals. People have ancestors and descendants who can be named. This list shows that Yahweh is not dealing with abstract linguistic, ethnic, or geographical categories. He is dealing with families who have ancestors. To later generations these ancestors were not shadowy, legendary figures but identifiable persons.

In verse 21 Miriam's name is added to an all-male list by the Greek Septuagint, the Samaritan Pentateuch, and by one manuscript of the Masoretic (standard Hebrew) text. Is this some sort of a witness to the gradual acceptance of women as persons in their own right in Israel?

Verses 25-27 round off the list with an almost dogmatic theological assertion that Moses and Aaron acted under Yahweh's express authority in bringing out a group of oppressed people "by their hosts," that is, virtually as a victorious army.

CONTEST
Exodus 6:28–11:10

There has been too much attention given to the explanation of the plagues as phenomena and too little attention given to their significance as events within the tradition of Israel's faith. There may well have been a series of natural happenings in Egypt that gave rise to the plagues described in the book of Exodus. All of them could quite feasibly have taken place in Egypt, though not in such a tight sequence. There might be a connection between the list of plagues and the lists of curses found in some ancient Near Eastern texts. The theological purpose and significance of the plagues, however, have a prior claim on our attention.

According to the tradition in Exodus, the plagues were sent in order to glorify Yahweh. They were sent to teach Egypt, Pharaoh, and the gods of Egypt (Pharaoh being regarded as a visible embodiment of deity) who was the real god. "The Egyptians shall know that I am the Lord" (7:5). They were sent to teach Israel that the God who had just made contact with them was acting in history and that they must trust him.

The very English word "plague" is misleading. It is a mistranslation of the word used in the standard Latin translation, the Vulgate. The Latin word, *plaga*, really means "blow" or "infliction." In the original Hebrew, the plagues are variously described as "miracles," "signs," or "wonders." They belong with the strong belief expressed in the Psalms celebrating the Exodus and in Gen. 18:14: "Is anything too wonderful for the Lord?" Of the fourteen psalms that contain some such celebration, two give a didactic list of the plagues (Pss. 78:11-12, 43-51; 105:26-36). The fact that there are striking differences in the number, description, and order of the plagues does not appear to have worried any of the Old Testament writers. For example, it seems more important to the author of Psalm 105 that the order of the plagues should correspond to the order of creation in Genesis 1. The idea of fixed and immutable "laws of nature," which even Yahweh will not break because he has made them, would not have occurred to the theologians of the Hebrew tradition. "Law" and laws derive from Yahweh; therefore, nothing he does is extraordinary or marvelous for him.

The basic message of the plagues is that through miracles, signs, and wonders Yahweh exposed the gods of Egypt, including Pharaoh, for what they were. At the same time, he convinced the Hebrews that they were his chosen people. They must therefore trust him to rescue them from oppression. The plagues are the demonstration in practical action of God's concern for this group of oppressed people, and, by extension, for all oppressed people and, indeed, for all humanity. They are also a battle of *creation*. Historically they may seem of minor importance, but theologically they have cosmic significance. Pharaoh threatens human life with his policy of ethnic cleansing. He is defeated by the God who employs the whole of creation from the mighty Nile to tiny insects.

6:28-30 These verses repeat 4:10-17 and presumably derived from a different source. The theology is the same, however, and reflects that of the overall author. We should not get lost in the literary sources, helpful though their tentative identification may be. Instead, we should try to discern what the final author is conveying, since this is our only reliable insight into the authentic faith of Israel.

7:1 "I have made you like God to Pharaoh." This is an incredibly bold challenge to the status of Pharaoh. Not only is Pharaoh's claim to divine authority dismissed along with that of Egypt and her gods, but a mere Hebrew, and one raised charitably in his own household, will wield divine authority over him! Aaron will be prophet to Moses. The classic word for prophet *(nābî')* is used here and shows the understanding of the basic role of the prophet in Hebrew tradition. A prophet may utter warnings and promises for the future, proclaim the way of social justice, or call

Israel away from apostasy. Nevertheless, the basic function of a prophet is to speak for Yahweh to his people just as Aaron speaks for Moses to Pharaoh. This double appointment of Moses and Aaron entails the significant claim that God may from time to time appoint his own representatives to speak on his behalf to the human leadership in the world, whether it claims divinity or not. As the people of Israel find out later in their history, the problem with prophecy lies in discerning the legitimacy of the prophet's claim to authority. Does he speak as God's genuinely accredited representative or does he merely claim to do so? In this passage, Pharaoh appears to accept Moses' claim while rejecting the authority of Yahweh that lies behind it. In the appointment of Aaron, we also see the prevalent custom, still operative in parts of Africa and the Pacific islands, of a spokesman (or "talking chief") being appointed to relay the messages of the chief or king.

7:3-5 Yahweh will "harden the heart" of Pharaoh, that is, make him obdurate or stubborn. In 8:15 and in other places Pharaoh hardens his own heart, but in 9:7 and elsewhere his heart "was hardened." In this latter expression, the agent is not specified, but we may assume that the formulation is a "divine passive," with God as the implied agent. Three different verbs are used, the one conveying the idea of "heaviness, obstinacy"; the other, of "being firm"; and the third, of "hardening." These different expressions may indicate different literary sources, or they may be deliberate changes in emphasis.

The text sometimes stresses the action of Yahweh, sometimes Pharaoh's obduracy. The notion that God would harden Pharaoh's heart has caused much trouble for Christian theologians, from Paul onwards, so much so that it almost seems that a Society for the Prevention of Cruelty to Pharaohs has been formed. The theological difficulty has even led to an archaeological search in Egypt for the mummy of a Pharaoh who suffered from cardiosclerosis in a literal sense! Such a ridiculous search fails to recognize that "hardness of heart" is a Hebrew idiom. In the context of the Exodus story, it stresses Yahweh's absolute control of the situation. It places the emphasis as much on Yahweh as Pharaoh, whose very resistance is turned to the promotion of God's plan. Pharaoh's refusals to listen are genuine refusals and conscious decisions. Each refusal makes the next one more inevitable. Yet their very inevitability cannot thwart the intentions of Yahweh. The ultimate aim of Yahweh's action, to which even Pharaoh's will (one of the many meanings of "heart" in Hebrew idiom) is subject, is that "The Egyptians shall know that I am the Lord" (v. 5).

Israel must learn that nobody can hinder Yahweh, and Pharaoh becomes the unwitting agent in Israel's learning process. Pharaoh, though, must demonstrably have a will of his own to show the power of Yahweh's will. Pharaoh exercises his will by intensifying his resistance, thereby making a habit of obstinacy. This is precisely what people do to themselves. What is often overlooked in concern for free will is that throughout history rulers have played at being God and have had to learn that they are mortal. At least Pharaoh was encouraged by long-standing Egyptian belief to consider himself divine. Other rulers have had less excuse. Nevertheless, their will cannot stand up against God's "great acts of judgment" (v. 4).

7:8-13   The main contest is preceded by a challenge. Pharaoh challenges Moses and Aaron, "Prove yourselves by working a miracle." The snake with which the contest begins is, in fact, called by a more general term (*tannîn,* reptile) in verse 9 (contrast 4:1-5). This again might indicate two literary sources. It also may represent a conscious echo of the myth of divine combat with a sea monster, which is found in several ancient Near Eastern sources (on *tannîn* as sea monster, cf. Gen. 1:21; Job 7:12; Ps. 74:13; Isa. 27:1; etc.). The dragon-slaying myth recurs in the New Testament (Revelation 12), in the European legends of St. George and the dragon, and in works of modern fiction like J. R. R. Tolkien's *The Hobbit.* If the word *tannîn* is intended to carry a mythological association, then Yahweh's representative would be taking on the sea or river dragon of Egypt and symbolically swallowing it up. Further, the contest with the Egyptian magicians, who normally would be expected to manipulate miraculous powers, would heighten the drama of a preliminary

41

contest between Yahweh and the gods of Egypt, a contest which must be settled first before the great act of liberation can take place.

In verse 11, the local experts are called "wise men," "sorcerers," and "magicians" (*hartummîm,* an Egyptian loan-word, evidently used for priests who uttered spells and incantations at funerals). Two of these magicians are given names in later Jewish tradition — Jannes and Jambres — and make their way into the New Testament (2 Tim. 3:8).

7:14-24 Ancient Egypt did not have the geographical box shape marked out in our atlases but consisted of a wide river with its banks and irrigable hinterland. It was a riverbank civilization, in which two fertile strips of riverine cultivation, interlaced with irrigation canals, supported a large population and a powerful unified state. For all its advanced organization and massive buildings, Egypt depended totally upon the waters of the Nile and the disc of the sun. So when the waters turned red, probably at the yearly time when the seasonal floods from the Ethiopian mountains brought down mud or vegetation from the Blue and White Nile, Egypt was disrupted, its daily life thrown into confusion. The symbolic meaning of the pollution of the Nile is even more impressive. The source of life for a mighty civilization is stricken and made to bleed. The bloody Nile itself becomes a sacrifice offered to the God of the Hebrews. The deity of Egypt is stabbed by Moses' rod and becomes the victim.

The fish in the Nile die (v. 18, 21). Even the sap from the trees and the water from the wells are affected (the words "vessels of" before the words "wood" and "stone" in v. 19 are an addition to the text; the intended meaning likely includes all water contained in wood or stone, not just bowls and jugs in houses). The disruption is now complete. What makes this even more pointed is that Pharaoh appears to have gone to the bank of the Nile for some religious ceremony, perhaps to bless the waters, like the blessing of the rivers in Cambodia that used to be performed by the king, or the "wedding" of Venice to the Sea, carried out when the Doge threw his ring into the Adriatic.

In verse 22 the magicians carry out the same transformation

by their arts, though how they do this when all the waters are already blood is not explained. The point is that the *contest* still continues; the devotees and experts of the gods of Egypt only succeed in adding to the disgrace and confusion.

7:25 Although the seven days that elapse between the first and second plague may simply stand for "a fair amount of time," they more likely recall the seven days of creation in Genesis 1. The theology of the book of Exodus implies that Yahweh as all-powerful Creator has absolute power over the world of Egypt.

8:1-15 The second plague, of the frogs, is now inflicted. An infestation of frogs would naturally follow on the pollution of the Nile and would cause great inconvenience, to put it mildly. Large numbers of frogs would have seemed sinister to the ancient Egyptians in the same way frogs do in some parts of Africa and toads do in parts of Europe. The religious implications of this plague lie with the Egyptian deities Hapi and Heqt, who were represented by a frog's head. Heqt was worshipped as the goddess who granted safe childbirth and thereby ensured the continuation of human life. Thus, the Egyptian deities claiming to control the essential power of human fertility are defeated through their symbols, the frogs. In verses 3 and 4 there is a graphic description of the invasion by the frogs of all human life. They swarm into the houses and lives of the Egyptians. A challenge is issued to the deities of birth by the God who grants all life. The local magicians only succeed in making matters worse and adding to the troubles of Egypt and her gods (v. 7), like the unhappy youth in Dukas's story in music, *The Sorcerer's Apprentice*, who imitates his master's magic and only succeeds in multiplying his problems. In contrast, Aaron wields his rod and exercises authority over the life of Egypt. After Pharaoh's pleading and Yahweh's relenting (vv. 8-13), there are two results of the plague. The land of Egypt stinks (v. 14), and Pharaoh, once the plague is safely over, again hardens his own heart (v. 15).

8:16-19 Piles of dead, stinking frogs could easily become the breeding places for the little insects that now afflict man and beast. The Hebrew word for these creatures, *kinnîm,* has been translated in various ways. The first-century Jewish philosopher and exegete, Philo of Alexandria, described them as creeping up noses and into ears. If he identified the right insect, then ''midges'' would be a better translation than the larger ''gnats'' (the understanding of the Septuagint and Vulgate translations). ''Maggots'' (NEB) could hardly be on both man and beast, whereas ''lice'' (Syriac Peshitta; *Targum Onkelos;* AV; RV) or ''sand fleas'' (RV margin) could easily be, but none of these renderings fits Philo's description. Whatever they were, the thrust of the plague is that by the ''finger of God'' (v. 19), Aaron strikes the ''dust'' (''soil'' is a better translation) of Egypt so that it produces its self-inflicted pestilence. Land, people, and gods are all struck together by Yahweh. The magicians lose out this time and are ignored from this point on in the narrative. Their power-lessness proves that Egypt is unable to help herself. All Pharaoh can do now is allow his heart to be hardened.

8:20-24   Pharaoh again goes to the river, to be met with the fourth plague, the ''swarms.'' In the Hebrew, we are not told what made up these swarms. The Greek Septuagint has ''dog flies.'' They must be more than the normal swarms of houseflies, dung flies, or bluebottles that infest hot climates. They could be gad flies or horse flies. It would be attractive to translate them as ''swarms of scarab beetles,'' since the scarab was the royal emblem of the Pharaohs and would add another ironic twist; as a plague, though, this would be a little far-fetched. Rather, the ironic twist lies in the exemption of the land of Goshen, where the Hebrews live (vv. 22-23), whereas the land of Egypt is ruined by them (v. 24).

8:25-32   The next interview with Pharaoh sounds like a piece of political negotiation, with neither side revealing its motives. Pharaoh wants to make sure that his labor force does not escape and insists that they remain within Egyptian territory to carry out their sacrifices. Moses claims that the Hebrew practices would offend the local Egyptians and would lead to the Hebrews being stoned (v. 26). The real objection underlies what Moses says to

Pharaoh, since he uses the sort of language that Pharaoh is likely to understand — the technicalities of the cultus. Moses does not want the Hebrews merely to sneak out of Egypt on some pretext or other, but to march out to meet Yahweh at Sinai. An exodus, not a furtive escape, will take place. Pharaoh again hardens his heart against the liberation of the people and the sovereignty of Yahweh.

9:1-7 The next plague strikes the domestic animals with an unidentified, but lethal, disease. This could be anthrax, or even something like mad cow disease, and could result from the previous infestations. In ancient Egypt, domestic animals were an extension of any settled community and essential to its livelihood. They were not seen as individual personalities, that is, as pets, but as part of the basic life of Egypt. Hence they and the supplies of food and clothing represented by them are threatened. The Egyptian gods, Apis, Ptah, and Ra, were all physically represented by bulls or calves.

The slaying of the domestic animals clearly shows that Yahweh has again triumphed over the gods of Egypt. The animals owned by the Hebrews remain unharmed. Camels, listed here (v. 3) with the other domestic animals and also mentioned in the stories of the patriarchs (Genesis 24), are not an anachronism, as some have declared. Camels were domesticated at Mari, in Mesopotamia, in the eighteenth century BCE, though they were not recorded as such in Egyptian records until much later. We should accept the allusion as being accurate and rather assume that the Egyptians themselves did not domesticate camels.

9:8-12 The "ashes" of the succeeding plague, and the "boils" they produce on humans and beasts, are something of a mystery. The word translated as "ashes" (NRSV "soot") occurs only here in the Hebrew Bible and may be connected with a verb meaning "to blow." Since the kilns would have produced pottery, lime, or charcoal, the ashes could be dust or soot. If there is a natural sequence from plague to plague, then the dead animals' carcasses have been incinerated, and these are the resulting ashes. At all events, the result is boils or sores, which, though not fatal, add to the usual skin problems of Egypt. With heavy irony, the local experts, the "magicians," are not only unable to compete, but are themselves afflicted. Neither Pharaoh nor the gods of Egypt can do anything about it.

9:12   At last, this time, it is Yahweh who hardens Pharaoh's heart, whereas up to this point Pharaoh has hardened his own heart. It is almost as if Pharaoh's repeated refusals have plunged him into an inevitable spiral of stubborn resistance. Yet Yahweh still gives Pharaoh a chance to change his mind.

9:13-35   At this point, the threat against Pharaoh himself becomes very pointed. (The word *heart*, in the phrase "to your heart" of v. 14, seems to have been inserted into the Hebrew text by some scribe, probably because of the repeated mention of Pharaoh's stubborn heart. It can easily be emended to "upon you" with little change to the consonantal text.) Any personal sense of security that Pharaoh might have had is removed. His divine authority cannot protect him from the God of the Hebrews. Throughout history, many rulers have become so accustomed to the powers they wield and of the rightness of their ideologies that they, in effect, make themselves into gods. Often after inflicting suffering on the people they rule, they eventually learn that they themselves are not invincible.

Hail is very rare in Egypt. It can be very destructive to growing crops and, if large enough, can endanger animals and humans as well. The Lord sends "such heavy hail as had never fallen in all the land of Egypt since it became a nation" (v. 24). The word *gôy* is used in the Hebrew Bible of any non-Hebrew people and is not a racist label. The word *'am* stands for Yahweh's chosen people, while *gôyim* stands for the rest of humanity. It is a theological, not an ethnic, distinction. Once again, Goshen is not affected.

In verse 27 the incredible happens: Pharaoh admits that he has sinned and that he and his people have done wrong. His attitude of repentance and humility contrasts with his previous brazen hardness of heart and with his subsequent defiance after the plague is lifted. It also contrasts with Moses' physical posture of standing erect and spreading out his hands in prayer.

Flax and barley (v. 31) ripen in January in Egypt, whereas wheat and "spelt," the coarser version of wheat also grown at this period, would not be high enough out of the ground to be affected by hail.

10:1-20   Locusts are a terrible infliction wherever they strike. Their sudden arrival, huge numbers, and relatively small size demonstrate painfully and obviously the utter impotence of Pharaoh, the Egyptians, or their gods to do anything at all to prevent or get rid of this plague. They have to sit helplessly by until the creatures decide to move on, leaving devastation and probable starvation behind them. The locusts pose no immediate physical threat to human beings, since they do not bite, sting, or even irritate. They can even be edible under different circumstances (Matt. 3:4). In verse 1, the message is sounded out loud and clear: Yahweh admits to having hardened Pharaoh's heart so that Egypt will experience the utter frustration of seeing its whole livelihood ruined. Egypt returns to chaos, the barren condition described in Genesis 2 before Yahweh provides water to make the ground fertile and fashions human beings to be stewards of his creation. Israel has to see for herself abundant proofs of the powerlessness of Egypt and her gods before she can accept the power of Yahweh.

Verse 2 is a clear theological statement showing that Israel's *tradition,* not just the historical record, concerns the writer. The writer assumes that the Exodus from Egypt is a series of historical events that actually happened. Far more important than that, it is a live tradition, actively convincing generations of Hebrews of the power of Yahweh. Yahweh, their God, has made fools of the most powerful nation known to them, and of the gods of that nation who had made it great. The true purpose of the plagues, the Exodus, and everything else is disclosed in the words "that you (and your descendants) may know that I am the Lord." Throughout the course of history, false gods, ideologies, and systems have proven foolish and have come to nought, sometimes by means of humanly uncontrollable events. As with the plagues of Egypt, the goal of history is still that the true God eventually be acknowledged and worshipped.

10:4   The Hebrew language has various words for locust (cf. Joel 1:4, 2:25), as do the languages of those countries that suffer periodically from them. Their names reflect the effect of the insect, rather than its taxonomy. Here it is the "army locust," carried from its breeding grounds in Arabia by an east wind, swarming everywhere in vast numbers, devouring every leaf, and then, just as suddenly as it arrived, being driven into the Red Sea (v. 19). The shape of the locust's head and its destructiveness led to comparison with the war-horses of an invading army (Joel 2:3-11).

10:6   To terminate this interview, Moses and Aaron turn and leave. Such an action would be an insult to an absolute monarch, who alone had the right to bring an audience to an end and before whom the suppliant was supposed to kneel and then back out. Pharaoh's advisers plead with him to cut his losses and rid himself of this threat to his authority and to the very life of Egypt by releasing the Hebrews (v. 7). But Pharaoh still wants to keep his grip on them. Only the males may go to sacrifice (sacrifice is often a male prerogative). The women and children must remain behind as hostages against their return. Hostage taking, as a form of blackmail, has always been a popular mode of terrorism. With that demand and with Moses' refusal to comply, Moses and Aaron are expelled from Pharaoh's presence, doubtless in retaliation for Moses' exit in verse 6.

10:17   Pharaoh confesses his *sin* against Yahweh. Sin, in this place, can only mean disobedience and rebellion. There is a wide meaning given to sin throughout the Old Testament. It cannot be narrowed down to liturgical omissions (e.g., failure to sacrifice or to sacrifice in the right way), as has sometimes been alleged on the grounds that such sins receive attention in the book of Leviticus and elsewhere. Nor can one claim that a moral or theological sense of sin grew out of a "primitive" liturgical failure to comply. We cannot date senses of sin. The sin for Pharaoh lies in his refusal to face the plain facts of the plagues — "this deadly thing" — and to accept Yahweh's power over him and over Egypt.

10:21-29   "A darkness that can be felt" refers to that blackness, heat, and pain caused by the stinging, blinding clouds of dust and sand whipped up by the khamsin wind from the south (a wind equivalent to the sirocco in France, the föhn in Austria, and the berg in southern Africa). This infliction upon Egypt also implies a threat of a return to the terrors of primordial chaos (Gen. 1:1). The Egyptian sun god, Amen-Ra, is shut out from the land he has created and which he maintains by a darkness and sand not of his own making. Life is threatened with the powerful symbols of chaos and death. This lasts for three days, the accepted period for certainty of death, the same period as for the burial of Jesus.

10:24   The Hebrews are now given their marching orders, but this time with the proviso that the animals belonging to them must remain behind as hostages. This is not a letting go at all. To begin with, for how long is a tribe of nomads likely to remain alive in the Sinai desert without their animals? Moses attempts to point out that they cannot offer sacrifices without animals to sacrifice, and they do not know yet how many animals or of what sort must be sacrificed. Moses' objections may sound like a refusal to go in for the normal methods of diplomatic bargaining. Nevertheless, he insists that *all* of Israel, including animals, must be liberated. Pharaoh has been asked to let Israel go. He must let go all of Israel, not portions of Israel, keeping back nothing, not even a hoof (v. 26).

10:28   All negotiation has now failed, and Pharaoh admits defeat by banishing Moses. Moses then replies in kind.

11:1-3   There is evidence from the Elephantine stele that the first Pharaoh of the Ramessid dynasty (Seth-nakht, 1185-1182 BCE) had to deal with a conspiracy in which Asiatics were involved. These people were eventually given a generous cash bribe and persuaded to leave Egypt. The taking of the jewelry from the Egyptians does not constitute a theft or a confidence trick but rather a symbolic action. Moreover, it is difficult to imagine it happening on a large scale, since the Hebrews did not have many

Egyptians as close neighbors. They had been allotted the land of Goshen away from the centers of the Egyptian population. Nor does the jewelry represent compensation for work done in slavery. It is rather a demonstration of the ancient practice of celebrating a victory by plundering the defeated. The Egyptian jewelry is a visible sign that Yahweh has won the "mother of all battles" over Egypt and its gods. Egypt is now paying tribute to the people of Yahweh. Later on the loot itself becomes tainted when Aaron melts it down to make the golden calf (Exodus 32). This is the only passage where the word "blow" is used for a "plague"; it has been reserved for the last and most severe of the afflictions. In verse 3 it is recorded that Moses gained great respect from the Egyptians, significantly more than from his own people.

11:4-10 The last plague arouses most concern in modern times, since children are the sufferers (though "firstborn" could have included males of all ages), as they are in the story of the babies slaughtered by Herod, when he was trying to eliminate Jesus. In these days, when so much public indignation is aroused by reports of child abuse, this is a predictable reaction to a totally different story from a different age. This sort of reaction, though, misses the point. The context is theological and liturgical, not moral and humanitarian. Deities were, and still are, offered the firstfruits. The first sheaf of corn from the field, the first lamb from the flock, the first bunch of grapes from the vineyard, the first libation of wine — all these were offered as sacrifices expressing gratitude and tribute. They were means of communicating with those superhuman powers whose bounty had provided both land and harvest. Decisively, then, Egypt and her gods and her semidivine Pharaoh are forced to offer firstfruits, both human and animal. This sacrifice is now offered to Yahweh, for he alone is God.

This movement of sacrifice culminates centuries later in Yahweh's provision of his own firstborn as the firstfruit offering of the whole human race. The offering of Christ is the decisive and ultimate sacrifice of the firstborn, in which God provides his own firstborn. Here we see the beginning of a long chain of tradition and faith. Egypt unwillingly sacrifices its firstborn to the

God of the Hebrews. This is the same sacrifice proposed to Abraham but not exacted from him (Genesis 22). In the Old Testament no more sacrifice of human firstborn will take place after the escape from Egypt. Instead of offering their own first-born, the Hebrews will offer a lamb for each family and will repeat this sacrifice yearly down the generations. The sacrifice of the firstborn, however, is still needed if total communication is to be achieved. This sacrifice was ultimately provided by the Father himself in the person of his Son. This sacrifice, also unrepeatable, is extended throughout the generations to the present time in the Eucharist. It is God's way of showing that he will provide the ram for the sacrifice. For now, though, the Hebrews must know, once and for all, by means of the last plague, that Yahweh is God. "He it was who struck down the firstborn of Egypt, both human beings and animals" (Ps. 135:8); he it was "who struck Egypt through their firstborn, for his steadfast love endures for ever" (Ps. 136:10).

The power and authority of Yahweh are linked throughout to his choice of Israel. The Israelites have to be convinced of this; otherwise, they cannot carry out his plan for them and therefore cannot be eligible to be chosen by him in the first place. The humiliation of Pharaoh and of Egypt's gods is secondary to this. The primary goal of the plagues is the supreme revelation of Yahweh to the Hebrews at Mount Sinai. On that event will depend Israel's future and God's ultimate plan for all peoples.

PASSOVER
Exodus 12:1–13:16

The origins of the Passover Feast in Israel are disputed. Only one factor is agreed upon by all: it is a very old festival indeed. The Hebrew name for the feast, *pesaḥ*, is something of an enigma in itself. The Hebrew lexica give three entries under the Hebrew root *p-s-ḥ*.

1. The verb *pāsaḥ*, "be lame, limp," is used in 1 Kings 18 of Israel's double and treacherous allegiance to two deities at once (v. 21) and also of the gyrations of the Baal prophets around the altar on Mount Carmel (v. 26). It is also used, with the preposition *ʿal*, in Isa. 31:5 of Yahweh protecting Jerusalem as a bird protects its young. This should not be translated as "hovering" (RSV), since no birds hover over their nests to protect their young, though they might well patrol them or swoop around them. Clearly some sort of irregular movement is being described in these different circumstances.

2. The adjective *pāsēaḥ*, "lame," is used of Saul's grandson Mephibosheth (2 Sam. 4:4; 9:13; 19:26) and of animals unfit for sacrifice (Deut. 15:21).

3. The noun *pesaḥ* is still used to this day for the Passover feast itself. Obviously, the name of the feast is linked with the verb or the adjective in Hebrew thought, in order to show that Yahweh skipped over and spared the Hebrew firstborn. Nevertheless, Hebrew derivations of words found in the Bible are not exercises in etymology but lessons in theology. They are pressed into service to convey theological truths.

The most widely accepted theory of the origins of the Passover is that it was a nomadic spring festival, which the Hebrews already observed before they arrived in Egypt (cf. the festival referred to in Exod. 5:1). It was a night celebration, held at full moon before the spring equinox. Unleavened bread and bitter herbs were desert fare and belonged to the celebration of the spring full moon, before nomads would begin their trek to fresh pastures. The feast of Unleavened Bread *(ḥag hammaṣṣôt)*, though usually referred to separately in the Hebrew Bible, was held at the same time as Passover. Unleavened Bread is thought to have been an agricultural feast fused with Passover at the time of the religious reform instituted by King Josiah in the seventh century BCE (2 Kings 23).

Whatever Passover's historical origins, the directions for its observance, repeated in Deuteronomy 16, make the meaning of this feast in Hebrew tradition quite clear. Whatever it had been, Passover was no longer a cyclical, seasonal event, marking only springtime or the new year. It was an essential part of the Exodus event, a living link between Exodus-Sinai and the ongoing life of the Hebrew community. Passover seems to have been forgotten for a time and then revived. For the Hebrews it became a *family* event celebrating and actualizing God's mighty redemptive act in history, and it was an act of sacrifice, looking back to the sacrifice of the firstborn and forward to the sacrificial system of the Jerusalem Temple.

Passover is the sacrifice that deals with God's actions for and in Israel at the Sea of Reeds. It is a thoroughly historical feast, not a cyclical fertility rite. The bondage under Pharaoh, the escape from Egypt, the miracle at the Sea, the saving and ransoming motifs — all find their place in Passover. In Israel we have the association of cult with historical event, with events seen and understood as having happened at a certain time and in a certain place. Assuming that a traditional seasonal ritual was adapted to the historical needs of the Hebrews, the way is open for us to consider the adoption of various religious practices by the Hebrews. The truth is that the people of Israel saw no problem in taking over customs and practices from their neighbors and from their kin.

Sacrifice itself did not originate with the Hebrews. Sacrifice is a worldwide practice common to almost all cultures and races. What, then, does it signify? It is an ancient practice through which relationship is established and maintained, and a communication between the human and the divine is carried on in material things. It is a means of converse between deity and humanity, in which the transferring of the thing sacrificed into the domain of the holy becomes the action through which divine-human conversation flows.

The Passover was a sacrifice. Animals were slaughtered by the community that owned them. Their blood was then exhibited as proof that life had been given over to the Holy God. His acceptance of the sacrifice was made known in sparing, "skipping over," the offerers' homes so that no sacrifice of firstborn was exacted of them. Their sacrifice culminated in a meal celebrated in the family setting. The relationship between Yahweh and his chosen people was thus sealed. These and other detailed liturgical instructions found in the latter chapters of Exodus emphasize the importance of ritual in Hebrew theology and practice. The people of Israel should remember what Yahweh has done for them, not only in renewed trust in him and in seeking justice in the community, but also in assiduous and obedient worship in the offering of sacrifice.

What we have in Exodus 12 is the whole Passover tradition in its final liturgical form. Succeeding generations adapted it to their needs, while retaining its essential character as a festival of liberation by sacrifice from danger and oppression. Its successor in Christianity is the Last Supper, which has the same essential character in a wider context of liberation.

12:1-2 The historical nature of Passover does not do away with its seasonal origins and meaning. Indeed, seasons in a large part of the world are more important than dates and hours of the clock. However, the New Year festival came to have a much deeper meaning; it became a festival of liberation, rooted in a historical event. The month of Abib (Exod. 13:4) was later called Nisan (Neh. 2:1) and fell in March/April, the time for the ripening corn.

12:3-5 The lamb (or kid, though traditionally the lamb became the norm) was a year-old sheep. As a family feast, the Passover was designed to feed ten to twelve participants. Small family groups could combine. Relationships were very important to the Hebrews. Hence, many of the laws, customs, and liturgies are aimed at relationships, especially those relating to the family. When, in the Deuteronomic reform (2 Kings 23) all sacrifices were concentrated in the Temple alone, the actual slaughtering was done there, but the feast was eaten, family by family, within a certain area of the city of Jerusalem, around the Temple. By Jesus' time this area included the whole city.

12:6 The lamb is to be slaughtered in the evening of the fourteenth of Nisan (Abib). The instructions say "between evenings," which means twilight, the normal time for a feast, since it became cooler and was an ideal time for a relaxed meal. This is the normal ambience for sacrifice the world over. A sacrifice is rarely a grim or solemn event, but a family meal, eaten in the presence of the deity in the cool of the evening.

12:7 This first Passover has a definite context — the escape from Egypt and the exemption of the Hebrews from the offering of the firstborn. The blood, here to be smeared in special places, is of the essence of animal sacrifice. Its use clearly shows that the life of that animal has been totally given over to Yahweh — "to the death." In passing, it is amazing that Protestant versus Catholic disputes over the sacrifice of the Eucharist can still influence scholars in their treatment of the Passover. Some scholars claim that the smearing of blood is not a sacrificial act, but the Passover certainly is a sacrifice and, once the Temple was destroyed, it became the only sacrifice practiced by the Jews.

12:8 The lamb is to be roasted over an open fire. For nomadic people, roasting would be the normal method of cooking meat and would allow the remaining blood to drip out. Since blood represented the life given over to the deity, it was regarded as holy and not for human consumption. The bitter herbs were originally those that grew wild in the semidesert and were used for flavoring. They came to symbolize the bitterness of former slavery. The unleavened bread, perhaps something like drop scones or griddle cakes, would have been baked on hot stones by the sun's heat. They came to be identified as the "bread of haste" because the Hebrews could not wait for the yeast to rise before escaping from Egypt.

12:9-10   This sacrifice is to be a *zebaḥ*, in which the whole animal is offered to God and the meat is eaten in celebration and in fellowship with Yahweh and with each other. Anything of the animal remaining uneaten or not especially sacred to Yahweh must be burned and thereby consigned to him.

12:11   The instructions concerning dress for the journey firmly anchor the Passover in the historical event of the escape from Egypt.

12:12-13   Yahweh will pass judgment upon Egypt and her gods. The exemption of the Hebrews and the provision of a sacrifice for them to offer instead of their firstborn is an echo of Genesis 22, where Israel's ancestor Isaac was exempted from being a sacrifice and a ram was provided in his stead. The event represented the first stage in the revelation of sacrifice at the heart of God, which was eventually fulfilled in the ultimate sacrifice of Jesus Christ.

12:14-20   Instructions about the future observance of Passover are woven into the narrative here. It is indeed strange that there is hardly any mention of a Passover being held in the history of Israel until King Josiah revived the feast as part of his reform program in the seventh century BCE (2 Kgs. 23:21-23).

Josiah's avowed aim was to eradicate all apostasy, all worship of any other god than Yahweh, and to bring his people back to the covenant in accordance with the commands proclaimed by the scroll discovered in the Temple (2 Kgs. 22:3-20), which most scholars identify as an early form of the book of Deuteronomy. The Passover symbolized Israel's history and life in faith. Josiah therefore revived the feast and celebrated it with great solemnity precisely because of its connection with the Exodus. He also transferred the actual slaughtering of the animals to the Temple to guard against any worship or sacrifices being given to any gods other than Yahweh. Heads of families presided over the feast, as provided for in Exodus 12, though priests carried out the actual killing of the victim. Ironically, Passover came into its own when the Temple ceased to exist. To this day, the Passover Seder remains the most impressive of Jewish liturgies.

12:14 The Hebrew word usually rendered "memorial" *(zikkārôn)* is hard to translate into Western languages, after centuries of Christian controversy over the Eucharist. So also is the Greek word *anamnēsis,* the New Testament and Septuagint translation of *zikkārôn.* The verb *zākar* is rarely, if ever, used in Hebrew of a purely cerebral activity, as the English word "remember" is used. Nor is it used of a simple commemoration, in the way that past leaders or writers are commemorated on the dates of their deaths or births. Nor, of course, does the word mean "to repeat." Clearly, the death of the firstborn was not to be repeated, and the escape from Egypt could not be repeated. When God "remembered" his people, he acted and *did* something effective for them. So when the Passover is described as a "remembrance" or "memorial" for all the years to come, it means that the liberation of the Hebrews from Egypt, once historically carried out, is to be actualized in the contemporary history of the present Israel. "All those wonders are *now* upon us, as we are," they could say about the Passover memorial. By Jesus' time, the Passover was *the* celebration of liberation and redemption for the Jews and had attracted into its liturgy a recitation of all the mighty works of God from creation onwards. For Christians, it is therefore no accident that, according to the synoptic Gospels (Matthew, Mark, and Luke) Jesus died at Passover and that his final Passover meal took the Passover "remembrance" forward into the future and outward to all peoples by means of his own sacrifice.

12:15-20 The instruction on the use of unleavened bread (taken up by Paul in 1 Cor. 5:7-8) became an insistence on a yearly fresh start for the whole community. The old leaven must be used up or swept out before the new leaven can be made and used.

12:21-28   Some scholars regard this section as an alternate, older tradition concerning the Passover (so NRSV note). Liturgical instructions are woven into the narrative. Hyssop (v. 22) is probably what we know as the herb marjoram, or origanum, a tall herb suitable for sprinkling water or blood. Moses instructs the elders that Passover will be "a perpetual ordinance for you and your children," (v. 24) with the head of the family answering the liturgical questions put by the youngster of the family (vv. 25-27).

12:29-32   The actual slaying of the firstborn in Egypt is one of the most horrifying events of the Old Testament. It provokes the question, "Does God kill babies?" First, it has to be pointed out that *all* the Egyptian firstborn, not just the infants, died that night. Secondly, the whole point of the story is not that Yahweh is ruthless, but that the Hebrews must learn, once and for all, that their God is all powerful and demands their total allegiance. The utterly willful oppression and resistance of Pharaoh leads Yahweh to show that he, the Pharaoh, is not God. Likewise the gods of Egypt are not gods. Instead, they have to be forced to offer sacrifice to the one true God. Pharaoh's capitulation (vv. 31-32), in which he actually asks Moses' blessing, amply testifies to this.

12:33-36   The Israelites leave in haste but in victory. Jewelry represents the normal spoils of battle. Since Yahweh has conquered Egypt and her gods, his people must collect those spoils.

12:37-38   The incredible number given (600,000 men in addition to women and children; cf. Num. 1:17-46; 11:21; 26:51) is clearly an exaggeration and is not meant to be taken literally. A "thousand" is a collective noun, indicating a sizeable cluster of people, a natural grouping rather than an exact figure.

A *mixed* group of people left Egypt. Racial purity and religious separation — ancient apartheid, if you will — developed much later, in the Exile in Babylon, (see Ezra and Nehemiah) and then as a protective measure against foreign cults and influences. It was not "the Israelites" as a distinct ethnic group who came out of Egypt and settled in Canaan, but "God's people," defined by grace, not race. The issue was fought out in the early Church, and exclusion on the grounds of race, language, or culture was banned. Nevertheless, discrimination or separation of some sort or other has continued to haunt the Church.

12:41-42 The Hebrews are called God's "army," his "host," even though they are unarmed and vulnerable, a mere rabble of refugees. The application of military epithets to the people of God recurs throughout both the Hebrew Bible and the New Testament.

12:43-49 In light of verse 38, admission to share in the Passover meal is not by qualification of *race,* but through involvement in the community of God's people. Hence, slaves circumcised into membership will be included, though they are not Hebrews by birth. The hired servants are not included because they have no intention of joining the people of God. Nor are the *gērîm,* sojourners in transit who remain on the fringe of Israel, unless they intend fully to join the community, in which case all their males will have to be circumcised. Ancient Israel never totally accepted a missionary vocation for herself, and proselytizing in later Judaism has always been a slow and unwilling process. Defining and maintaining boundaries never involved, least of all in the escape from Egypt, a deliberate policy of apartheid, with one race keeping itself apart from others and oppressing or exploiting other races. Later on in Hebrew history, a policy was developed of protecting Israel from foreign gods and cultic practices hostile to Yahweh. The Hebrews were a people set apart for Yahweh, until there could be another great act of liberation, a bursting free of the constraints imposed by a very real fear of reversion to the cults and gods of the ancient Near East. So for the time being, uncommitted passersby were not allowed to share the Passover meal.

12:46-47 Passover is to be an undivided feast. The animal must be roasted *whole* and no bones are to be broken. The feast will be celebrated by *all* Israelites. *All* the families of the Hebrews are united in celebrating Passover together, with their *one* Lord and God. The *whole* of Israel eats *whole* roast lamb on *one* specific day in the evening, in the presence of the *one* God, whose mighty act of liberation they are witnessing. Israel is labeled the *ʿēdâ* — "gathering, company, congregation" — called into being by Yahweh himself. Israel is a community by virtue of God's call, not by virtue of ethnic origin or political necessity or common interest.

13:2   The general instruction for the offering of the firstborn has been put into the context of the last plague. This is to be the last offering of the human firstborn, until the offering of Christ as firstborn (Col. 1:15).

13:3-10   Once again, the day is to be "remembered," with all that the verb conveys, especially when the Hebrews come into the Promised Land. There they will be among other peoples worshipping other gods, and they are to remember that Yahweh alone is the all-powerful and that he is the one who brought them up from Egypt. They will be in an agricultural, settled community, where bread is normally made with leaven. Therefore, they must then eat unleavened bread to remind them of the escape from Egypt by the power of Yahweh.

13:5   The list of the inhabitants of Canaan, which appears with variants in many places (Exod. 3:17; Deut. 7:1; etc.) is not simply a piece of ancient ethnography. The lists do not necessarily reflect ethnic groupings. The label "Canaanites" probably indicates all the peoples living in the lower part of Canaan. The "Hittites" were the remnants of settlers from the times of the Hittite Empire, many of whom were ethnically Indo-European, not Semite. "Amorites" is a general term for hill dwellers. The "Hivites" may have been Hurrian settlers. The "Jebusites" were the tribe indigenous to the Jerusalem area (2 Sam. 5:6-8). The listing of these peoples underscores the power and grace of Yahweh in giving the Hebrews at least some areas of Canaan; it also evokes the threat posed to Hebrew religion and faith by so many alien cults.

13:11-16 The firstborn are to be "set apart," a technical term for sacrifice (cf. 2 Kgs. 16:3; 23:10; etc.).

13:13 Human firstborn males are to be "redeemed," that is, bought back from their real owner, the Lord. Certain animals and their firstborn are also to be redeemed. The context of the last plague must again be kept in mind.

13:9, 16 The Passover and the offering of the firstborn are "signs" on the hand and "memorials" on the forehead. They are visible tokens of the Lord's power and love exhibited in the Exodus. In later Jewish tradition, these terms came to be taken literally, and pieces of parchment with Scripture passages came to be worn as signs of dedication to the Lord and to the Torah (cf. Deut. 6:8-9). Many observant Jews continue the custom of wearing these "tefillin" or "phylacteries" today. Originally, though, these terms referred to the sacrifices themselves, Passover and the offering of the firstborn, as signs of God's power.

ESCAPE
Exodus 13:17–15:21

The escape from Egypt is a faith event. It is *the* crucial event of the whole Hebrew tradition. It is also the source of all the biblical language about salvation and liberation, including the theology of the Cross. Its importance for Christians, as well as for Jews, cannot be exaggerated. Since its importance is chiefly theological, we should begin not with its historicity but with its theology. To take this approach is not to imply that the actual historical facts, if they can indeed be verified, should be ignored, but to recognize that in the eyes of Hebrew faith the escape from Egypt happened just as it is recorded in the Torah. From this point certain themes emerge:

1. The escape from Egypt is the responsibility and initiative of the God of the Hebrews. In this event, Yahweh keeps his promises to the patriarchs, creates a people for himself, and punishes Pharaoh and the gods of Egypt.

2. The actual historical details, though important to those of us with a Western training and background, have a low priority in the story as a whole. The overriding concern is with what Yahweh does with and for his newly adopted people.

3. All that precedes and follows in the biblical narrative is taken up into this event and given meaning by it. It is a cosmic event, and cosmic language is employed to describe it. In the tapestry of human history, this event may appear to be only a few stitches of faded thread. For the faith of the Hebrews, however, it is the event of the universe. All Hebrew ancestry leads up to it, and all subsequent Hebrew history flows from it.

4. The group of Hebrews rallied round Moses is no revolutionary movement. Moses is certainly the chief human actor in

the drama, but the author, director, and producer is Yahweh. The Hebrews are indeed liberated, but the main aim is not just to set them free, but to set them free for a purpose: to become the people of Yahweh.

5. The Hebrews do not fight in their own cause; they are not allowed to do so. They do little physically to help themselves and nothing by way of aggression or even self-defense. God does the fighting, and nature is his ally — water, fire, cloud, the plagues, the whole cosmic panoply. This signals the beginning of a theology of nonviolence that reaches its culmination in the Old Testament in the Servant Songs of Isaiah 40–55 and that dominates all other theologies of human action when it reaches the New Testament. God will fight for his people, not they for themselves. Eventually that fight will culminate in the Cross of Christ.

6. The escape from Egypt creates a new society, in which a group of slaves becomes a community, a nation. Their polity, leadership, and government bear no relationship to any system of that time and can be summed up in the word "theocracy" in its purest sense ("rule of God"). Yahweh rules.

7. Moses is the ideal and prototypical prophet. With Moses as Yahweh's mouthpiece, communication between Yahweh and his people takes a new form. Yahweh establishes his inalienable right to raise up his own agents, to endow them with his spirit, and to deliver through them his messages to his people. Moses' designation as prophet par excellence indicates clearly the role of the prophet in Israel. All aspects of leadership are derived from Moses and owe their origin to Yahweh.

8. Descriptions of the various aspects of the escape, some of them different from the account in Exodus, are given in some of the Psalms (e.g., Psalms 74, 77, 78, 80, 99, 114) and in the prophetic literature (e.g., Hos. 11:1; 12:9-13; 13:4-5; Zech. 10:11; Hag. 2:5). More significantly, the language of escape, redemption, liberation, and ransom occurs repeatedly throughout the Old and New Testaments. Jesus is hailed as the new Moses who redeems (Luke 1:68; 2:38; 21:28; 24:21; Rom. 3:24; 8:23; 1 Cor. 1:30; Gal. 3:13; 4:5; Eph. 1:7, 14; Col. 1:14; 1 Pet. 1:18; Heb. 9:12, 15; Rev. 5:9), ransoms (Matt. 20:28; Mark 10:45; 1 Tim. 2:6) and sets free (Rom. 6:18, 22; 8:2). The language

used is deliberately the same as that used to describe Yahweh's massive and seminal act of liberating Israel from Egypt.

13:17   The escaping Hebrews do not leave by way of the military route into Canaan, which came to be called "the Way of the Philistines." The use of the term Philistines may be an anachronism, since the Philistines themselves landed in Egypt at the beginning of the twelfth century BCE. They were refugees from whatever disaster overtook the Minoans in Crete, and they reached Egypt via the outer Aegean islands, only to be driven away from the Nile delta and to settle on the coastal plain of southern Canaan.

A greater problem is posed by the crossing of the "Red Sea" (13:18). As is well known, the Hebrew text reads *yam sûp,* "Sea of Reeds." At the level of historical analysis, it would seem most likely that the Hebrews escaped from Egypt via the marshy pans near the present day town of El Qantara, where the Suez Canal is now, thereby avoiding the Egyptian garrisons that guarded the normal route for travelers from Africa to Asia. Their crossing would have been at the southern end of Lake Menzaleh, which is one of the shallow, seasonally fluctuating lakes in the isthmus. This route would be consistent with the wind that dried up or drove aside the shallow water but left mud to clog the pursuing chariots and put them at the mercy of the returning floods. Nevertheless, we cannot just write off the Septuagint translation, which speaks clearly of the *Red Sea.* After all, the translation is very old, and "Red Sea" would have been an unlikely substitute for the geographically more plausible "Sea of Reeds." It may well be that the Septuagint translators were making a theological point in insisting that the Hebrews crossed the natural barrier between Africa and Asia, the Red Sea, and that Pharaoh and all the gods of Egypt could not cross that barrier.

There is a mythological level to the story that describes a historical event as a pure act of God, not an act of people or natural forces. The language that is used transports the whole event into the realm of myth as well as that of history. The story is a variation of the ancient myth of the conquest of evil by good, in which the forces of nature take part. Therefore, far from being a historical embarrassment, the Song of the Sea in the next chapter places the escape from Egypt firmly within the context of God the cosmic deliverer (cf. Ps. 74:12-15). Small wonder, then, that the Exodus has been appropriated as the very type of all liberation. Yet from this event, the whole concept of liberation expanded and changed. Liberation was never supposed to be restricted to one group of people or to a purely social, political, or economic area of life. The ending of the Song of the Sea (15:18) says just that.

13:19   Joseph's bones are taken with the Israelites into the Promised Land. This act has symbolic significance beyond that of showing respect for the ancestor. Abraham, Isaac, and Jacob all live on in Israel's land and are thus physically heirs to the promises once made to them. The promise made to Joseph (Gen. 50:25-26) has been fulfilled. The solidarity and continuity of the family and the respect for Joseph's bones contrast with modern clinical ways of treating remains.

13:20-23   From now on the Hebrews will be a pilgrim people, living in tents, but they will be a people with an identity. The word *sukkôt*, the name of the place from which the people set out, means "caravansary." They are led and protected all the time, by day and by night, not by guides, guards, and guns, but by Yahweh. The pillars of cloud and fire in the narrative could well have been inspired by a camp brazier or even a distant volcano, smoking in the daylight and glowing in the dark. Here they represent the visible assurance of Yahweh's protection, the sacrament of his presence. They continue the theophany of the burning bush. The whole of the Exodus story is focused on Yahweh's revelation of himself. He hears, he liberates, he guides, he protects, and, at Sinai, he *is*.

14:1-4   The Hebrews are caught encamped on the Egyptian side of the "Sea" and Pharaoh again hardens his heart. This is necessary for the final defeat of Egypt's gods. The Egyptians must know that Yahweh is God.

14:5-9   Egyptian chariots, like modern tanks and planes, had a statutory crew, consisting of a driver, a warrior, and a navigator.

In all likelihood Pharaoh sent a small detachment to round up these stray refugees and did not lead the expedition himself. (He is not mentioned as being involved in the disaster.) The account speaks of 600 "picked" chariots and all the rest of Pharaoh's chariots. If we were to envision this scenario in contemporary terms, it would be like having all the tank regiments of the U.S. army, plus any other mechanized units available, sent out to apprehend a bunch of untrained, unarmed refugees encumbered with noncombatants and trying to escape across the Mexican border! The point is not the likely exaggeration of an obscure historical event, but the proclamation that Yahweh, without human aid, has defeated the superpower of the ancient world, including that power's pretension to divinity. "All the king's horses and all the king's men couldn't put Egypt together again."

14:10-14   The "murmuring" begins. Israel is not merely passive, but actively resistant to Moses and to its savior God. With the Egyptian army in sight, the thrill of escape soon wears off. Yet the Israelites must learn the meaning of faith. In Scripture, to have faith in God means to place your trust in God, and not just to acknowledge his existence. The pattern of murmurings throughout the journey reflects the difficulty humans always have in letting God take over. This resistance corresponds to Pharaoh's hardening of his heart. It also makes it abundantly clear that the Exodus is not about replacing dictatorship with democracy. The narrative as a whole does not see the Exodus in purely political or social terms. Furthermore, there is no evidence of a *widespread* popular movement of liberation throughout the Near East at that period. To read such a situation into the text here would involve a procrustean exegesis. Yahweh, and not any "glorious revolution," is the subject throughout. When God acts, despots harden their hearts, and people murmur and refuse to trust him.

14:15-29   The ordeal of the Israelites continues when they face the water. They are forced to rely upon the power of Yahweh over nature, mediated by Moses and his rod. Wind and waves obey him, as centuries later they do Jesus on the Sea of Galilee. There is no need to imagine huge walls of water on either side of the road, towering above the Hebrews. The "wall" of water signifies protection from attack. The expression is not intended to describe an architectural feature but represents a vivid use of pictorial language to describe the reality of a safe and protected path. At Yahweh's command, the water protects the Hebrews and destroys the Egyptians. The Hebrew and the Greek both try to solve the mystery of what happened to the chariots. The Hebrew says that the wheels were "turned" (twisted off?). The Greek says that they were "bound" (stuck in the mud?). Whatever happened, the narrative depicts a dramatic scene in which God calls upon the forces of nature to rescue his people.

14:30-31   The verbs in verse 31 express the purpose of the whole operation.

- Israel *saw* the great work,
- the people *feared* (gave respect to) the Lord,
- they *believed* in the Lord and in his servant Moses.

15:1-18   The "Song of the Sea" or "Song of Moses" is not just a piece of primitive poetry inserted into the narrative out of respect for its antiquity. Antiquarian respect alone would not have secured its place in the final version of the book of Exodus. It may well be very old, but it functions in the narrative to show one of the main reasons the Hebrews were delivered from Egypt: so that Yahweh would be revealed as cosmic king. This is what the poem proclaims. It shouts out loudly that the God who has acted in liberating his people from oppression must be honored and worshiped. The biblical theme of *holy war* begins here. Yahweh will see to any fighting that has to be done. Any victories won are his victories. Yahweh reveals himself in ways other than that of the divine warrior. In Isaiah 40–55 he commissions his servant (and Israel) to suffer and be a sacrifice for his people and for all peoples. The Song of the Sea also celebrates a cosmic dimension to Yahweh's victory. This echoes the language used in ancient Near Eastern myths of chaos, particularly those of Ugarit. As in the first chapters of Genesis, the scenario here differs significantly from its ancient Near Eastern parallels. First, the Exodus is not a battle between matched gods, but the victory of the one Yahweh over all opposition, human, divine, or natural. Second, the sea here is not the embodiment of chaos but an instrument in the triumph over chaos. Third, the kingship of Baal, the Canaanite warrior god, gives way to the kingship of Yahweh. Fourth, both in the Song and in Psalms 74 and 136, Yahweh is the sole Creator of all that is. We may discern, then, a close connection in theology and in language between the creation of the world (Genesis 1–2) and the creation of the people of God. Throughout the Song, Israel remains passive. There is also no mention of the pillars of cloud or fire. The whole emphasis falls on Yahweh's unaided mighty acts. In the New Testament, the Exodus theme is again taken up in the book of Revelation (Rev. 15:3). There the crystal sea replaces the Red Sea, the elders replace the Israelites, and the Beast replaces the Egyptians. The Song shows the response expected from the Hebrews, which is the very essence of the response to God in faith: (1) they see and experience his mighty acts; (2) they fear and trust him; (3) they trust his appointed agent; (4) they praise him; (5) they serve him with sacrifices; (6) they recount his mighty acts. "Leave v. 4 aside, and what God has done could be made generally applicable to God's work everywhere. This is a Creator God who is at work in this way all over the world. No wonder the other nations are trembling" (Fretheim, *Exodus,* 163, 166).

15:1-3   Just as the "I" in many of the Psalms speaks for Israel corporately, so here Israel praises Yahweh as one person.

15:4-12   These verses celebrate Yahweh's victory at the sea by adapting divine-warrior imagery from the common stock of ancient Near Eastern religious language (cf. Ps. 78:12-13). The language is deliberately macrocosmic and vividly anthropomorphic. It defines Yahweh as no mere tribal deity but as the creator God. He stretches out his "right hand," piles up the waters with the blast of his "nostrils," and blows with his "breath" or "wind" (Hebrew *ruaḥ*). Another stock motif from ancient Near Eastern religion that has been adapted here is the notion of a council of gods: "Who is like you, O Yahweh, among the gods?" (v. 11). In its earlier stages,

Israelite religion acknowledged the existence of the gods of other nations but, in a practical monotheism or monolatry, insisted that Yahweh, the creator of heaven and earth, was supreme over all deities. The divine council motif appears elsewhere in Gen. 1:26; Deut. 32:8-9 (NRSV); Psalms 82; 89:5-7.

15:13-17 These verses not only memorialize the victory at the sea but also celebrate the entry into Canaan as a past event. At first glance, Yahweh's "holy abode" (v. 13) and "sanctuary" and "mountain" (v. 17) would seem to refer to Jerusalem/Zion, as in many of the Psalms (e.g., Psalm 87) and would therefore bring the composition of the song into the period of the monarchy at the earliest. If this is the case, then there is a deliberate linking of the Exodus with the promise of stability for the people of God, living around the visible sacrament of his presence, the holy city and the Temple. Although Jerusalem may have come to be understood as the referent of these terms, however, their prior referent would be the cosmic mountain of Canaanite mythology, Zaphon ("North" in Hebrew; cf. Ps. 48:1-3 and the NRSV note there).

The word *ḥesed* is used to describe Yahweh's loving relationship to his people. It occurs in the midst of the more aggressive language of the Song and was to become a favorite expression in the writings of many of the prophets, such as Hosea. The Hebrew word is very difficult to translate into modern English, since its semantic area includes loyalty, faithfulness, and caring as well as genuine love. Another key word is the Hebrew verb *gā'al,* translated as "redeem." Unfortunately, in popular English usage, the word is largely restricted to the act of buying back articles from a pawnbroker. Its Hebrew meaning is to take responsibility for someone who is in some sort of serious trouble. As such it is used in the famous passage in Job 19:25 ("I know that my Redeemer lives"). Thus does Yahweh take responsibility for his people.

15:14-15 The list of enemies — Philistines, Edomites, Moabites, and Canaanites — belongs to the period of the Judges and the early monarchy. The Egyptians do not appear in these two verses.

15:18 This verse is a liturgical shout, or acclamation, similar to those in Pss. 93:1; 96:10; 97:1; and 99:1. It could have been used at the annual enthronement festival of Yahweh, enthroned in the person of his deputy, the king, in the Temple.

15:20-21 The dancing of Miriam and her companions would probably have been similar to the rhythmic swaying and singing that can still be seen and heard today in parts of Africa and Asia. It expresses freedom of spirit in freedom of movement and in shared rhythm. It expresses praise and joy. This dancing poses a stark contrast to that of the golden calf episode (Exodus 33), just as Miriam's role here contrasts with her rebellious role during the desert sojourn (Numbers 12). Because of her role in this ecstatic reverie, Miriam is called a "prophet." The Song of Miriam in v. 21 is widely recognized to be one of the most ancient of poetic couplets in the Hebrew Bible. The newly formed people express their freedom by praising their liberator God. They are no longer slaves. They belong to Yahweh and to nobody else.

ON TREK

Exodus 15:22–18:27

The long journey begins. Long journeys are standard fare in the traditions and epics of many cultures. The Vikings sail across the North Atlantic; African tribes migrate across half a continent; Dutch *voortrekkers* set out from the Cape; Mao and his comrades make the Long Walk. In *The Lord of the Rings,* the Nine set off for Gondor. Jesus journeys as an infant to Egypt and back, and Paul sails for Italy and eventually arrives at Rome. It is not so much the distance that is significant, as the hardship, the sense of purpose, and the fulfillment of the promise awaiting the travelers at the end of the journey. The trek of the Hebrews has all of the hardships associated with long, arduous journeys — hunger and thirst, the threat of hostile forces, an inhospitable landscape. But there are also safe stopping places, oases, and friendly visitors. The journey to the Promised Land is a thrilling epic about a people who have to learn to trust their visible leader, Moses, and their invisible leader, Yahweh. "So the people feared the Lord and believed in the Lord *and* in his servant Moses" (14:31).

Liberation from Egypt is not followed immediately by the meeting with Yahweh at Sinai; nor is it followed by an instant transit to the Promised Land. Instead, the Hebrews escape from Egypt into a different situation of threat, the wilderness. The experience must have been rather like that of a long-term prisoner in a modern jail being released into a society where all the familiar landmarks are replaced by unfamiliar ones, leaving him exposed and vulnerable. Hence it is small wonder that, from the beginning, the people murmur and rebel. The wilderness experience was later idealized by Jeremiah (2:2) and Hosea (2:15) as a honeymoon period in which the Hebrews responded obediently, eagerly, and

71

lovingly to Yahweh. The Exodus narrative, like parallel accounts in Pss. 78:17-42 and 95:8-11, tells a different story — murmuring right from the beginning and throughout the whole journey.

The Hebrews exhibit a recurring pattern of behavior as they plod on. Their need for food, water, and some degree of infra- structure — things that were provided for in Egypt — becomes acute. So they murmur. They direct their murmuring at Moses, but in so doing they reveal their lack of confidence in Yahweh. They are threatened with punishment, because, in spite of their experience of being liberated from Egypt, they still do not trust Yahweh. Moses then intercedes for them. Yahweh once again answers, forgives, and meets their need. This cycle is repeated often in Israel's subsequent history. Indeed, the cycle is basic to the theological understanding of Israel's history reflected in the Deuteronomic history that stretches from the book of Joshua through 2 Kings. This cycle of unbelief, the theologians of Israel could see, was the real explanation of the vicissitudes of their history and even of the major disasters such as the Exile. The cycle is illustrated in the experience of individuals as well. The pattern recurs in Elijah's journey to Mount Horeb (1 Kings 18).

Jesus' wilderness experience represents the culmination of the journey through the desert. Life seen as a journey to the Promised Land is a spiritual reality for the people of God, whether as a community or as individuals. Sometimes they march; sometimes they plod wearily on; sometimes they linger, depressed; sometimes they stride with renewed hope. As they go, they mature in trust. There has to be a journey; otherwise, there is no arriving in the Promised Land.

15:22-25   *Marah* means "bitter," because the water at the oasis is undrinkable. Yahweh makes it drinkable by means of a desert bush of some kind. This is often overlooked as the first miracle of providing the water essential to life before the striking of the rock. It is taken up and paralleled by Elisha's action in 2 Kgs. 2:19-21.

15:26   A warning and a promise are conveyed, both to be repeated frequently. Murmuring and rebellion are typical of God's people, whereas restoring, forgiving, rescuing, and healing are typical of God. Whatever the people do and however they are punished, God's purpose is to heal them and restore the relationship.

15:27 The name *Elim* means "terebinths" or "evergreen oaks," and the place has been identified as Wadi Gharandel, which is sixty-three miles — a good three-day journey — from Suez. The twelve springs and seventy palm trees reflect the twelve tribes and the seventy elders. (In biblical theology, numbers are the servants of theology rather than the masters.) Together they indicate that the people of Israel have found their first safe haven prepared specially for them.

16:4-5 The petition in the Lord's Prayer, "Give us today our daily bread," like so many of Jesus' teachings, is clearly based on this event in the Exodus narrative. "Bread," *leḥem*, stands for food, basic food needed to provide for ongoing life. The Hebrews have been complaining that at least they had had food in Egypt. Evidently, they have forgotten that they were fed so that they could labor effectively on Pharaoh's monuments. God's reply promises a rain of food from above. He will feed them as his own liberated people, for nothing in return but obedience. Just as human obedience was tested at creation by the prohibition of eating from the tree, so also the Hebrews' obedience is tested by the prohibition placed on the gathering of food. They must trust the Lord to provide enough for their needs on the previous day. The extra day is, of course, the Sabbath (cf. vv. 22-30). Will they celebrate the Sabbath as their Creator does, by abstaining from the work of gathering up the food, which in any case will not be provided on that day? Or will they distrust him?

This passage speaks to a vital contemporary issue. It is an issue that applies especially to consumer-driven Western society. The accumulation and stockpiling of goods and the achievement of affluence are seen by some Christians and Jews alike as a sign of God's blessing. The motivating force behind this acquisition has been dubbed "the Protestant ethic," as if hard work and business acumen should be rewarded directly by the Almighty. This is *not* the message of the Old or New Testament. Daily bread means the basics in food, water, and clothing for the day, not luxuries for years to come. Biblical economics stand in contrast to the economics of our day, in which one section of the West supplies the rest of the world, at great cost, with vast quantities of arms with which to kill each other and keep the population down. There are killing fields instead of manna and quail fields. The Hebrew goal of every one sitting under his vine and his fig tree means what it says, not every prosperous person sitting guard over a mountain of rotting figs and tanks of wine, while thousands in other parts of the world have neither figs nor wine but only the daily prospect of death by guns from the West. There is something very wrong, if not downright offensive, about the prosperity cult, particularly if it is attributed to the teaching of the Torah.

16:6-10   As in the feeding of the five thousand in Jesus' ministry, there is a twofold purpose here. God miraculously provides food to meet a very practical need. Yet he does so to remind the people that he is the one who brought them out from Egypt and that they must still trust him. This event is therefore a theophany, a revelation of the glory of God, not just a miracle. "Glory" has become rather a debased word in English. The Hebrew word for glory, *kābôd,* can mean "weightiness" and can carry with it the sense of power, honor, or authority when applied to a person or, preeminently, to God. The Hebrews were given a strong sense of Yahweh's power and presence by the arrival of the food.

16:11-13   Quails are local migrants and are not strong fliers. They sink down exhausted after a day's journey, when the heat turns to cold in the desert night. We need not restrict these birds to the quail species alone, since many species of partridge or francolin or even sandgrouse are edible and are found in the area. Indeed Psalm 78 calls them simply "birds" and has them arriving after the manna. The reference to the dew may refer to the habit of sandgrouse of storing drops of water among their feathers when at a pool and then flying off waterlogged to their roosting place.

16:14-15, 31   The writer explains the name "manna" as an interrogative preposition turned noun: "What is it?" Whether this is sound etymology or not, it emphasizes the mystery of the food. Whatever it is, Yahweh has provided it. It is described as a "flaky" thing, but that word is found only here in the Old Testament and could also be translated "powdery" or "granular" or even "crisp." The traditional explanation of the phenomenon is that certain scale insects feed on the tamarisk tree and produce yellow or white granules, which are formed at night and can be gathered from the trees in the morning. These granules are rich in carbohydrates. Yet, once again, we need to look for the purpose of the miracle, rather than seek a natural explanation. Exact historical or botanical details have long since been lost or conflated or enlarged upon in the course of a long oral tradition. The theological significance of the manna is that Yahweh alone answered his people's complaint and fed them in ways that neither Moses nor they could have engineered for themselves. The timing and extent of the miracle also matter, as they do in the feeding of the five thousand (Mark 6:30-44 and parallels). We miss the point entirely if we think of them as merely "picnic sharing" situations. God demonstrates his power by feeding his people. By the time of the New Testament, the manna had come to be known as the "bread of heaven" (John 6:31-58).

16:16-26   An omer (a tenth of an ephah) represents the basic ration per person. Both losing out and hoarding are excluded. Yahweh will provide sufficient food for a day's sustenance. Nobody goes without, and if anyone attempts to stockpile the manna, it breeds maggots.

16:27-30   There are many theories concerning the origins of the Hebrew Sabbath. In its essentials it was unique. Whatever its possible nomadic, agricultural, or astronomical origins, the Sabbath day became a weekly witness to the tradition of Israel. It was a *celebration* and never a day of enforced boredom. Theologically, it signified dependence on God, obedience to him, and a special relationship with him.

16:32-36   The pot of manna is preserved so that it can be taken to the Promised Land, where it will serve as a visible reminder of God's power, a sort of inert sacrament of a life-giving event.

17:1-7   In Gen. 2:6 God provides water for his creation. A very unusual word is used there, translated by the English word "mist" or "fountain." God gives this water so that life may be possible to all. In the Exodus journey, not the word but the means of receiving water — from a rock — is unusual. It happens at Rephidim, somewhere in Sinai. This time, once again, the people murmur and challenge the Lord. Moses is instructed to use his staff, the emblem of his authority, to strike the rock. When he used his rod to strike the Nile, the water supply was rendered dead. This time, in the desert, he strikes the dead rock and it produces life-giving water. Geologists tell us that subterranean streams can be separated from the arid surface by a thin layer of rock. Once again, though, the thrust of the miracle is not geological but theological. God provides for his people as he does in creation, by causing life-giving water to issue from a deathly desert. In allusions to this event in Ps. 78:20 and Ezekiel 47, water flows from the new temple. Jesus refers to himself as the living, life-giving water (John 4:10-15; cf. 7:37-39). When Paul refers to the rock, he draws on a Jewish legend that enlarged the Exodus story by turning the rock into a traveling source of water, one that accompanied the Hebrews on their journey, thereby supplying them with water continually. Jesus, according to Paul, is himself that water, bringing life to humanity (1 Cor. 10:4).

The names of the places where these things happened, Massah and Meribah, are etiologies and theologies in themselves. The verb *māssâ* means "to test," and this is just what Yahweh does with his people after they do the same with him. The text relates the name Meribah to the Hebrew noun, *rîb,* often used by the prophets to describe a dispute between Yahweh and his people, the "murmuring" that continued throughout Hebrew history.

17:8   The Amalekites were evidently related to the Edomites (Gen. 36:12) and were traditional enemies of the Hebrews (1 Samuel 15; Deut. 25:17), even though they also were of

Semitic stock. Incidentally, their hostility undermines the theory
that Israel emerged out of a popular struggle against an estab-
lishment. Here, at least, we are dealing with local tribal feuds.

17:8-13   Moses upholds the Hebrews. His rod, in turn, is
upheld by Joshua and Hur. This is not a switching on and off
action, a magical use of power. It is a clear demonstration to the
Hebrews, who at that time were totally unused to desert warfare,
that, when attacked, they must rely on Yahweh alone to preserve
them.

17:14-16   The general meaning of these verses is clear, despite
the reference to the "book" and the strange name given to the
altar. They are memorials and witnesses to Yahweh's protection.
Presumably the name of the altar — "The Lord is my banner"
— and the words of Moses — "My oath upon it" (REB) or "a
hand upon the banner" (NRSV) — mean that, if the Hebrews
are attacked, either by human enemies or by snakes (Num. 21:8),
they are to rally to Yahweh as to a banner or flagpole. The result
of the battle is perpetual hostility against the Amalekites (v. 16).

The engagement with the Amalekites is an early example of
"holy war" waged by Yahweh against the oppressors of his people.
This theology needs to be examined afresh (see further the comments below on Exod. 23:20-33). As with any nation, the Hebrews and their descendants, the Jews, have a long and eventful
history, which includes many acts of aggression, many acts of
self-defense, and many periods of oppression by other nations.
Because of this, the Old Testament has gained a reputation,
particularly among those who have never studied it, for being a
catalogue of wars and brutalities.

This reputation is undeserved, since various theological explanations are put forward within the Old Testament itself. Two
theological considerations in particular are worth bearing in mind.
First, although Yahweh often protects his people, fights for them,
and eliminates some of those who would have eliminated them,
he does not always come to their aid. He sometimes punishes his
people by withdrawing his protection and leaves them at the
mercy of their enemies. The paramount example of this is when

Yahweh allows the people of Judah to be defeated by the Babylonians and sent into exile. Second, the theme of holy war against other nations should not be viewed in isolation from the theme of Israel's *vocation for the nations*. This is a theme that emerges in the Torah and the Prophets. Israel is called by Yahweh. He is not merely their own tribal god, but the Creator of heaven and earth. He not only takes responsibility for the nations (and all creatures) that he has made, but also bears responsibility for them. He calls the Hebrews out of Egypt, defends them against those who from time to time oppress them, yet reminds them forcefully that they have been called not only for their own sake but *for the nations*. This theology of vocation emerges already in Genesis, particularly in the accounts of God's covenant with Abraham, and finds its fullest expression in Isaiah 40–55. In those chapters, the vocation of Israel for the nations is clearly set out in the vocation of the Servant, a figure who represents both kingship and nationhood in Israel. Positively, Israel is called to be a light for the nations (Isa. 51:4). Negatively and painfully, Israel is called to suffer (Isaiah 53).

We should not, then, view the theme of holy war in isolation but see in the whole history of the Hebrew people their voyage of self-discovery as the people of God. In the course of that voyage, nationalism and exclusivism are, at times, given the sanction of being Yahweh's policies, at least for that particular time and place. Yet the Torah clearly states that God created and sustains humankind as a whole. This belief continues to be fundamental in both Judaism and Christianity. From a Christian perspective, the vocation of God's people being a light to the nations and suffering on their behalf has been fulfilled in the gospel of Jesus Christ.

18:1-12   The biblical record gives confusing and conflicting information about Moses' father-in-law. Here his name is Jethro (cf. Exod. 3:1; 4:18), but in Exod. 2:16-18 he is called Reuel, and in Num. 10:29 and Judg. 4:11 he is called Hobab (as in the Greek text of Judg. 1:16). Here he is a Midianite, whereas in Judg. 1:16 he is a Kenite, the leader of a tribe which is credited with showing kindness to the Hebrews during their wilderness sojourn (Num. 10:29-32; cf. 1 Sam. 15:6). The final authors and editors of the Hebrew Bible did not bother to reconcile these conflicting traditions. Jethro provides an *ʿōlâ* (whole offering) for sacrifice. This is certainly an emphatic "communion in holy things," showing peace and friendship, sealed and ratified in sacrifice in a covenant of blood.

18:13-27   The Midianite chieftain or priest, Jethro, lays the foundation of Israel's judicial system by his timely advice. This advice is accepted as advice from God. Once again, an obscure non-Hebrew tribe has influenced the development of the Hebrew people as the people of God. The form of government appointed by Yahweh for his people is a theocracy, in which the real ruler is understood to be Yahweh himself. Power and authority are then delegated to human leaders: Moses, then judges, and later, kings. These various leaders have to instruct the people, lead them, and judge between individuals and between clans. Monarchy, when it eventually emerged in Israel, was never intended to be a dictatorship. It was to be sacred, because it represented Yahweh to the people. Thus Moses and his successors, the judges and kings, had to mediate both between Yahweh and his people and between people within Israel. This task, as Jethro foresaw, was too much for one person. On Jethro's advice, power and responsibility are shared and leadership is both delegated and made collegial. Yet this is not a democracy. The "will of the people," though sometimes — and often disastrously — exercised by the tribesmen of Israel, is just as foreign an idea to Hebrew Scripture as "the will of Moses" is. What rules and leads the people of God is the will of God, accepted and implemented among his chosen people by the ministry of Moses and his elders.

This development in Israel's organization is expressed in terms of *tôrôt* — "decisions," "statutes," and "laws." Perhaps this is inevitable. Relationships tend to be expressed in terms of rules that must be kept, interpreted, circumvented, or bent. Basic to the Torah is the relationship between Yahweh and his people and among his people. Thus Jethro's advice prepares a ragged and complaining people for their next and greatest experience, that of encountering their liberator God.

SINAI

Exodus 19:1–20:21

Psalm 68 says, "Let God rise up . . . The earth quaked at the presence of God, the God of Sinai" (vv. 1, 8). The sheer personality of Yahweh burst forth upon the Hebrews. This bursting forth took place at the mountain called Sinai. There the God of creation confronted the Hebrews whom he had liberated from slavery. He told them in no uncertain terms who he was, who they were, and what their relationship with him was to be.

The giving of the Law at Sinai gave Israel her character and identity. It is no wonder that the New Testament regards Jesus as the fulfillment of all that happened at Mt. Sinai. The Mount of Transfiguration (Mark 9), where Jesus appeared with Moses and Elijah, represents Sinai revisited and has the double purpose of reaffirming the importance of Sinai and of revealing Jesus. The Exodus tradition claims that God revealed himself through Moses to the Hebrews. Out of this encounter came the Torah, which was to shape the life of that community and subsequently, through Jesus, of the whole human race. All this began in earnest at Sinai. This claim, far from being denied, is totally accepted in New Testament theology and, therefore, by the Church.

It is possible to recognize two origins for the faith of Israel, each associated with a mountain, Sinai and Zion. These two traditions have been woven together in the Hebrew Bible. An example of harmonizing the Sinai and Zion traditions can be found in Psalm 68. The Psalm begins with a magnificent vision of God (El or Elohim) emerging in all his power as a victorious conqueror. Sweeping away all opposition, he rights all wrongs. Then a challenge is issued to the various mountains of Canaan to accept the utter superiority of Mt. Sinai. This is a declaration of the lordship of Yahweh over all other gods. Yahweh proceeds to another superior mountain, Zion, which has its geographical location within Israel's allotted land. Once established there, he is worshipped in his Temple. All the nations, even Egypt, his people's former oppressor, will sacrifice and submit to him as their God.

Incredible! In the space of a few verses, we are taken from a mysterious and awesome supernatural event, at the foot of an unidentified mountain, to the Temple in Jerusalem. The psalm then claims that the God of Mt. Sinai has also set apart the hill of Zion as his holy place. The God of these two mountains is the Creator. His will must be obeyed; his principles must be followed, eventually by the whole of humankind. At Sinai and then on Zion, Yahweh says to Israel, "I am the one God who created you, who chose you and liberated you. I take you to be my people. Do you take me to be your God?" It is therefore significant that the exact location remains a mystery. All that surrounds Yahweh is mystery, especially the choice he makes of people, places, and times.

The faith of the Hebrews is founded upon the experiences described in the book of Exodus. Even if we could plot the map references accurately, and even if we could trace the various source documents or oral traditions, it would make very little difference to that faith. As far as the Old Testament is concerned, there is *one* tradition of faith. This is what the Hebrews believed about themselves, and this is what Jesus believed. This does not mean that Old Testament research is irrelevant or sacrilegious. Far from it. Scholarly research greatly adds to our understanding of how and why Israel received her faith.

It is possible that, hidden behind the story of Moses' dealings with his father-in-law, Jethro, there lies the worship of one god by the Kenite tribe. It is possible that a New Year Festival took place every year at Jerusalem at which Israel solemnly renewed her covenant with Yahweh. It is likely that various literary sources concerning the Sinai event were conflated during the Exile. It is possible that there were originally two traditions of faith in preexilic Israel, one focused on Yahweh's election of Israel and giving of the covenant at Sinai, the other centered on the security God provided for his special people in Zion-Jerusalem. These traditions were not two political ideologies opposed to each other, one democratic and the other monarchical and elitist. The biblical text presents one unified tradition in which previous beliefs have been so effectively merged and reconciled as to have become inseparable. (See J. D. Levenson, *Sinai and Zion: An Entry into the Jewish Bible.*)

During times of trouble, people tend to cling to what is already there, rather than formulate a new theology. To take a recent example, in Stalinist Russia the Orthodox Church did not produce a radical new theology or formulate new liturgies. Indeed, as Rolf Rendtorff states explicitly in his recent book *Canon and Theology,* the object of theological study is the biblical text, not a reconstructed history or a restored text. Much of the Old Testament was produced in its final form by and for a people in exile. They felt themselves to be in danger of losing their very identity and therefore clung to the theological tradition that they knew.

In Cecil B. de Mille's film, the Ten Commandments are etched by fire upon slabs of stone while Moses watches in wonder. They come fresh from God's own hand. Yet there are striking resemblances between the material in Exodus 20 and various ancient Near Eastern codes of law, especially those of the ancient empire of the Hittites. Archaeologists have opened up a whole new world of a dominant people in the Near East in the early Old Testament period. The Hittites conquered most peoples in the region and even posed a great threat to Egypt. They dictated treaties to those they conquered. Two copies of each treaty were made, one for storage in their own temples and the other to be kept in the temple of the subjugated people. Hence they are referred to as *suzerainty (overlord)-vassal* treaties. This practice was not limited to the Hittites, and it provides an analogy for the covenant formulated between Yahweh and his people at Sinai.

This gives insight into what actually happened at Sinai. It can be assumed that two copies were made of God's commandments, written on slate. These two slates were the size of those used in fairly recent times by schoolchildren. They were not huge slabs of stone.

The treaty document would originally have been terse in wording, and portable. Through the years a certain amount of commentary was attached to the basic form, and it is this developed form that we have before us in the book of Exodus. These commentaries are not journalistic verbosity but thoughtful application by theologians underlining God's will for his people. In ancient times, people celebrated the making or renewing of treaties not by a signature and a handshake but by the offering of sacrifice. In the book of Exodus, the covenant (Exodus 34) has become separated from the giving of the Ten Commandments (Exodus 20). They would, in fact, have been inseparable. The commentary (Exodus 21–33) represents a later fleshing out of the way in which the Torah was applied to every area of life.

Hittite treaties had appended to them a formidable list of blessings and curses. These were the sanctions of the gods, considered to be far more powerful and binding than military strength. Such sanctions do not appear in Exodus 20. They are found only in Deuteronomy 28 and Leviticus 26.

If we compare the form of the ancient Near Eastern treaties with the Sinai covenant, we note that the identification of Yahweh, the overlord, comes first (Exod. 20:2). Next comes a list of stipulations and conditions demanded from Israel as vassal. Taken with the covenant sacrifice of Exodus 34, there is a striking parallel with the ancient treaty forms.

It is the differences rather than the similarities that are significant and essential to an understanding of the faith of Israel. In ancient Near Eastern treaties, a king was the overlord, whereas here Yahweh is the overlord. Further, Yahweh liberates rather than conquers the Hebrews. He does not reduce Israel to the level of a subject people but constitutes them as his people, creating them out of nothing. His relationship with them is total, covering every area of life. This is expressed specifically in worship and in the quality of relationships within the Hebrew community.

The Hebrew prophets, from Elijah onwards, proclaimed to later generations what they knew to be the genuine faith of Israel. From Sinai, Hebrew religion was taken northwards to Canaan. There the Hebrews joined up with some of the Canaanite tribes, who recognized in Yahweh of the Hebrews their own senior god, El. Those Canaanites also related to the one God. This was the

God of the covenant, commanding righteousness and justice in their new social order.

The Sinai covenant differs from other treaties and codes not only in its form and content but also in its priorities. The giving of the Ten Commandments does not dominate the biblical account of the Sinai event. Nor does the sacrifice that concludes and seals the covenant. Nor even does the act of liberation that leads to Sinai. Instead, the theophany — the self-revelation of Yahweh to the Hebrews — dominates the Sinai event. Yahweh constitutes the event by his appearance. Yahweh makes a holy mountain, a holy people, and a holy Torah. Sinai is an explosion of God. It is no accident that Sinai, both according to the biblical tradition and according to any possible geographical location, is *outside* the Promised Land — independent, as is Yahweh himself, of all known theological territories. The very elusiveness of Sinai as a place contrasts with the absolute assurance of Yahweh's presence. The faith of Israel would not be disturbed if Sinai were never definitely located. But Israel's faith would evaporate into thin air if Yahweh were shown to be a creation of the human imagination.

Israel did not produce the Torah either by her own efforts or by the ingenuity of Moses. The Torah and the Ten Commandments owe their importance solely to the God who appeared at Sinai. This is what the tradition of Israel itself says. The language used in the Ten Commandments is unusual, if not unique. To begin with, the negative commands are expressed with finite verbs and the particle *lō'* ("not," as in "You shall *not*") instead of with the usual *'al* with the imperative. This means that principles, not mere prohibitions, are being stated here. Furthermore, no punishments are prescribed at this point, which is highly unusual. The Ten Commandments do not comprise a detailed law code but deal only with general principles. The word *apodictic* covers the absolute commands and prohibitions typical of the Ten Commandments, in contrast to the *casuistic* laws, which deal with specific conditions and cases. This means that Yahweh "laid down the law" or dictated the terms for living. When Stephen called the Ten Commandments "living oracles," he was expressing their true force and meaning (Acts 7:38). He claimed that they were now fulfilled and encapsulated in the person of his master, Jesus. This claim angered Stephen's hearers and led to his death. His hearers would have been more angry had they been told that the Sinai relationship was no longer theirs exclusively but was extended to all peoples.

In the Sinai covenant, God declares himself to his people and inaugurates a relationship with them. Centuries later he declared himself to all peoples and offered his forgiveness and love to them all. Sinai proclaims the will of God and the prescribed way of life for the people through whom he will reclaim all the world's peoples for himself. Sinai begins the dialogue of the Creator God with his creation. At Sinai, God says for the first time in recorded history, "Relate to me in worship and obedience, and relate to each other in respect and care. Thus learn the meaning of love."

19:1-2   There are three principal candidates for the location of Mt. Sinai:

1. Jebel Musa, at the southern end of the Sinai peninsula. On the northwest slope of Jebel Musa stands St. Catherine's Monastery, which was built on the orders of the Byzantine Emperor Justinian in 527 CE. One tradition that affirms this identification goes back to the fourth century CE.

2. In northwest Arabia, near the biblical land of Midian, where Moses settled for a while after his initial flight from Egypt (Exod. 3:1; 18:1).

3. In the vicinity of Kadesh-barnea, which has the advantage of being a three-day journey from the Nile Delta and of being closely associated with the entry into Canaan (Deut. 1:46).

Another candidate, proposed recently, is Har Karkom at the northern limit of the Sinai peninsula. Over 890 locations of ancient dwellings, including a small early Bronze Age temple have been discovered on this plateau, which overlooks the Arabah. A well-defined winding trail leads up from the villages below to places of worship on top. The whole area seems to have been abandoned in the twentieth century BCE. It could well be the sort of mountain — lonely and uninhabited, but with a reputation as a former place of worship — that would attract a group of escaped slaves to come apart and meet their liberator God.

19:3-6   Forceful and vivid language is used here. Moses appears as the intermediary between Yahweh and the people. This role in no way conflicts with the traditional roles of Moses as lawgiver and prophet. The impression is often given nowadays that Moses was among the great initiators or reformers of history. Yet in the Pentateuch Moses is not portrayed as a great lawgiver. Nor does Moses resemble any of history's great liberators or revolutionaries. Moses is not displayed before us as a Mahatma Gandhi or a Nelson Mandela. Rather, he resembles a spokesman for a chief. The ideas are not his, and even the delivery is at times entrusted to Aaron. True, Moses has the power to make or mar the message if he does not cooperate. The Sinai event is, nevertheless, Yahweh's event.

In their effort to render Sinai and other biblical events plausible, some interpreters place far too much emphasis on human initiative. The Bible does not do that. Our world is increasingly dominated by the initiatives of politicians, scientists, and bureaucrats. This is particularly noticeable in the West. The modern Westerner looks for the will of God only when something deemed unfair happens. God therefore becomes a celestial dustbin instead of a liberator. The Israelites, by contrast, looked for divine responsibility for the things that happened to them.

Through Moses, God addresses his people as "the house of Jacob" and "the Israelites." Yahweh and his people are tied to each other by their theological past and their theological solidarity. This is not done to exclude all others or to create more divisions in humankind, but to give the Hebrews their needful theological identity as the people of God. This identity, since it transcends all human divisions, will eventually be open to all human beings.

The metaphor in verse 4 of chicks being carried effortlessly on the back of the parent eagle vividly expresses support, strength, and protection. All that the chick has to do is to stay in place. All that is expected of Israel is that she remain obedient to her God. She will then be carried as she was in the wilderness.

In verse 5, the Hebrew word *sĕgullâ* gives the sense of a treasured personal possession (see Deut 7:6, 14; 14:2; etc.). The Hebrews, then, are special to God, with the condition attached that they "obey my voice and keep my covenant." Choice by

God has often been misunderstood in terms of privilege or favoritism. The result has been that those who think themselves to be chosen have attempted to keep the privileges exclusively to themselves. They have felt cheated when those privileges have been lost or when others have been included without their consent. Nationalism is dangerous. Christian nationalism is lethal, especially for Christians!

The expressions "priestly kingdom" and "holy nation" (v. 6) are used again in Isa. 61:6; 1 Pet. 2:5, 9; Rev. 1:6; 20:6. They are corporate expressions, applied to the Hebrews collectively. By calling the Israelites a "priestly kingdom and a holy nation," Yahweh endows them with certain qualities and tasks. First, there is kingship, which means that together they must give leadership. Second, there is priesthood. Together they must offer sacrifice and demonstrate corporately the holiness and distinct nature of God in their way of life.

19:7-9 From the thick cloud of glory, God converses with Moses. This is characteristic of the dealings that God has with human beings. Transcendence and immanence come together. God is wholly other yet intimate, both near and far. Such intensely creative tension is typical of biblical language.

19:10-15 The crucial encounter is about to take place. Moses warns the people as they encamp at the foot of the mountain. They are to be holy for Yahweh, specially set apart for him. On the third day, Moses tells them, they will meet with their God. They must wash their clothes; they will stand clean before him. They must keep away from the mountain itself, for it is dangerously holy and will mean sudden death to all who touch it. Only when the trumpet sounds the call to worship may they approach. Finally, the men must keep apart from their wives, in order to be at Yahweh's sole disposal.

19:16-25 The mountain is convulsed by a thunderstorm or a volcanic eruption. The first reaction of the people is to quake with fear (verse 16). Indeed, according to the Septuagint text *they,* and not the mountain, quake in verse 18.

20:1-2   What a daunting introduction to the Ten Commandments! The personal pronouns "I" and "you" dominate the whole proclamation. "I" is Yahweh, the overlord, who proposes the terms; "you" is the Hebrews, who may accept or reject those terms. Yahweh identifies himself as overlord. He challenges the Hebrews. He reminds them of his historical identity. He is the God "who brought you out of the land of Egypt, out of the house of slavery." This phrase is used 124 times in the Old Testament and leaves them in no doubt as to who they are: liberated slaves, owing their freedom and their very lives to Yahweh.

20:3   The first commandment, "You shall have no other gods before me," makes a theological, not a philosophical demand. It does not speculate whether there are any other gods and, if so, how many. It states a categorical demand that total allegiance is the choice put before the Hebrews after Yahweh's act of total liberation. "Before me" (literally, "to my face") should be translated more sharply as "in defiance of me," or "in opposition to me," or even by the English idiom "to my face" (as in the expression "He insulted me to my face"). Yahweh demands a one-to-one relationship excluding all other deities. Translated into practical terms for Israel, the demand means, "Offer no sacrifice to any other god." All worship belongs to Yahweh alone, and he will brook no opposition. In the twentieth century, the commandment means, "You shall have no other priority in life before God." The first commandment is just as relevant today as it was at Sinai and much more frequently rejected.

20:4-6   An image, *pesel,* represented the presence of a god among his devotees. It could be made of stone, wood, or metal, and its shape showed the chief attributes or spheres of influence of that deity. Hence the bull, so often found as an image for Baal, conveyed both his strength as a mighty warrior and his fertility. Rarely have people believed that gods actually reside in or confine themselves to images. A sacrifice placed before the image of a god was thought to be highly effective in gaining some benefit from the god. The sacrifice was expected to influence the actions of the deity. The ban on images in the second commandment is a ban on any attempt to control or limit Yahweh by making an image of him and thereby influencing him. Israel must understand the nature of her God and must not attempt to manipulate him. The commandment was never intended as a ban on all carved or sculpted objects connected with worship. In fact, neither sacred household objects (e.g., the *terapîm* of Genesis 31), nor the high priest's ephod (Exod. 28:15), nor the brass snake cast under Moses' orders (Num. 21:9) were seen as defying this commandment. Nevertheless, this commandment has often been misunderstood, with dreadful consequences. One example from church history is the Iconoclastic Controversy (from the Greek *eikonoklastēs,* "image-breaker") of the eighth century, which resulted in an incalculable loss for the history of art. Paintings, statuettes, and carvings can function as "windows into heaven" (a phrase used by John of Damascus to justify the use of icons). They need not be made into objects of worship or used to manipulate God but can be aids to worship and spirituality.

In any case, God already has an image — humankind (Gen. 1:27). To worship an image and to offer sacrifice before it is to place a totally unnecessary intermediary between the divine and the human and to undervalue the worth of men and women created by God.

What does it mean to say that God is "jealous" (v. 5)? Perhaps a better translation than "jealous" would be "full of zeal." The Hebrew word does not have the petty, insecure overtones of the English word "jealous." It describes a close, passionate, exclusive relationship, which is what Yahweh demanded of Israel. Here the term jealousy is drawn from the sphere of marriage. Yahweh demands exclusive devotion and will tolerate no rivals.

The prohibition against worshipping images is followed by a warning of judgment and a promise of blessing (vv. 5b-6). The temporal indicators — punishment to the fourth generation and blessing to the thousandth — are not to be taken literally. Rather, the statements express in vivid terms that God's judgment on disobedience is limited, whereas his blessing on obedience is unlimited. God rewards covenant loyalty and devotion with his own "covenant fidelity" — the sense of the Hebrew word *ḥesed,* often rendered "lovingkindness" or "steadfast love."

20:7 In Semitic cultures, names had meaning and power. Names of gods were thought to be especially powerful and, when used as curses or blessings, were expected to be immediately effective. In Jewish tradition, speaking the proper name of God has always been forbidden. However, this commandment forbids a specific use of Yahweh's name — that of trying to manipulate him. It does not refer to the use of his name as an unthinking swearword. The Hebrew construction requires a stronger English translation than "in vain," such as "maliciously" or "for evil ends" or "wrongfully" (cf. NRSV). Yahweh cannot be manipulated by means of his name. Christians should pray *for* people or causes and let God decide *how* to answer their prayers.

20:8-11 The origins of the Sabbath are lost in the mists of ancient history. It may have derived from the lunar calendar, and it may have come from Babylon. It could have been adopted by the Hebrews at various periods in their history. What matters is that, in the final shaping of the Hebrew tradition, the Sabbath signified far more than a day of the week or a holiday break. Someone has called the Sabbath a "holy space, a sanctuary in time." It was as holy as the Temple, which was a sanctuary in *space.* Just as a holy place provides a space for celebrating God and praising him, so does a holy time.

More specifically, the Sabbath was a day set apart for celebration, not for misery. It was not a day for which fasting was prescribed. There were other occasions for solemnity and repentance. This day was a "golden" day, not a "grey" day. In it the Hebrews celebrated two great events. First, they celebrated creation, proclaiming their worship of the God whose unique power had created and continued to create an ordered world in which time (seen in terms of a seven-day week and the various seasons of the year) was a secure dimension. Second, they celebrated their liberation from Egypt (Deut. 5:15). This was a sharp reminder that their origins were servile. They had belonged to Egypt and had been subjected to a hopeless drudgery with no end except by death or exhaustion. They were now free and, as a sign of that freedom, did no work on one day in the week. Instead, they were to relax and worship the God who had set them free to live in his world. Domestic animals, servants, and aliens shared that freedom. The celebration of both creation and liberation became part of the theological tradition of Israel.

The Hebrews are to "remember" the Sabbath. The Hebrew verb *zākar* means far more than the English word "remember." In the present context, the Hebrew word conveys the notion of mindful, careful observance or reenactment. It is used of the Passover, and its Greek equivalent, *anamnēsis,* is used in the New Testament of the Lord's Supper (1 Cor. 11:24). The Hebrews are to keep this space in their week in order to live in the faith of God as creator and liberator. This they are to do no matter what happens to them, whether on the banks of the Euphrates or in the flames of Auschwitz.

The Christian Sabbath is, of course, celebrated on a different day of the week. The "remembering" is still the same, though. Christians are to take one day off each week in order to celebrate and apply to their lives what God has done for them in raising Jesus Christ from the dead. Thus for both Jews and Christians, the Sabbath is the sacrament of God's rest.

20:12 The Hebrews may or may not have been concerned to divide the Ten Commandments neatly into two groups of five each — five for Yahweh and five for the neighbor. The ongoing life and faith of Israel depended, humanly speaking, upon the growth of the family. After all, apart from the family there were very few other means of passing on teaching. Few could read, mass media were nonexistent, there were no schools, and public instruction (aimed primarily at males) does not seem to have taken place until the Exile. Hence respect for parents involved respect for what they stood for and for what they taught. Both Exod. 20:5 and Ezekiel 18 are concerned with the solidarity of the generations, the one with continuity from the parents, the other with the responsibility of each person to keep faith with God even if the parents fail to do so. The converse of this continuity is the generation gap, which would have been not so much a threat to the fabric of society as a threat to the identity and faith of Israel. How could Israel know herself to be God's people if the older generation had not witnessed his mighty, saving acts or if its witness went ignored? The commandment to honor father and mother brings teaching on the family into strong relief. Throughout the Bible, God, creation, and families are linked together. To be sure, the family of the biblical teaching was a far more extended affair than the nuclear family of the modern Western world. Although the Old Testament shows a clear preference for monogamy, biblical teaching does not seem to be threatened by episodes of polygamy or concubinage. We do not find any apologies being made for Abraham's or Jacob's marital or extramarital conduct. Even Solomon's harem is condemned only because it led him astray to worship other gods. Both Testaments show a concern for divorce. "Alternative families" get no mention at all, not because couples living together or liaisons between individuals of the same sex were unknown, but because they were not families. Though such arrangements might have obtained from time to time, they played no part in the life of the community. It is no accident that Judaism has always stressed the family. It is likewise no accident that Christians know God himself as a "family." They do not see the Trinity as a projection of human family life, but view the godhead of Father, Son, and Holy Spirit as the archetype from which the human family is derived. The command to honor father and mother, along with the teaching of Genesis 1 and the New Testament teachings of Jesus and Paul, shows that the family is basic to the faith of Israel and thereby to the Judeo-Christian (and Islamic) tradition as a whole. This does not exclude growth in understanding and fresh insights concerning the roles of both the sexes. In the relationship of the people with God and with each other, the family is an act of creation essential to the human race.

20:13 The verb *rāṣâ* is always used in the Old Testament of "illegal" killing. It applies to the slaying of personal, family, or clan enemies; to the settling of old scores; and to the pursuit of vendettas and feuds. It is not used of killing in battle or of executions after the death sentence has been passed. Respect for a fellow member of the community means that his life must not be at risk from his fellow Israelite. A theological claim is also being made: it is God's prerogative to take life, since he created it in the first place. Only divine sanction (which war and a death sentence were sometimes seen to have) can decide who may or may not be deprived of life. Recent events have shown that this commandment is just as necessary in this century as in preceding ones and just as necessary in one culture as in another. Whether terrorism is perpetrated by the state, whether it be one shocking murder of a single person or the "ethnic cleansing" of masses of innocent people, the command "You shall not murder" still applies. No amount of sanitized terminology ("cleansing," "purge," "friendly fire" and other callous euphemisms) can delude us into thinking that ours is an advanced age with no need of this commandment.

20:14   Adultery is committed by married people or, at least, by one married partner. Fornication — sexual activity involving unmarried people — is dealt with elsewhere in the Torah. The distinction between adultery and fornication is made in many contemporary cultures. There are, of course, many unanswered questions attached to this commandment. Were women originally seen as property and therefore discriminated against by this commandment? In other words, was there a double standard, males being allowed, if not expected, to be unfaithful, while females paid for their infidelity with their lives? If so, at what point in Hebrew history did equal treatment for the sexes begin to be considered? Was the death penalty imposed in cases of adultery and, if so, was it seen as a sacrifice (a human sacrifice) to ward off Yahweh's anger from the community as a whole? What again of non-Israelites, especially slaves?

However discriminatory the commandment may have been in its original application — and even if the commandment was originally more concerned with paternity than with sexual mores — it did lay the foundations for a wider and deeper understanding of God's will for society. The incident in John 8 of the woman taken in adultery shows Jesus' attitude. He did not immediately search out the other party and demand that both be punished.

He did not excuse the incident as merely a "night out." He did not advise divorce proceedings. He upheld the commandment ("Do not sin again"), while introducing the prospect of forgiveness and of commuting the punishment. The priority for him was that the sanctity of marriage should stand above all other considerations.

20:15   "Whoever kidnaps a person . . . shall be put to death" (Exod. 21:16). This law, coming so soon in the text after the commandment, "you shall not steal," probably points to the original aim of the commandment. The sale of Joseph by his brothers (Gen. 37:28) provides a striking example of what would today be called the "slave trade" in which *people* are stolen. In Gen. 40:15 Joseph says very poignantly to his fellow prisoners, "In fact I was stolen out of the land of the Hebrews." As the community developed, theft of property, particularly of animals, was included, though this was dealt with by restoration. If the commandment had its origins in the slave trade, then a great deal is being said about the value of human life in a free community. A person may not be treated as a commodity, since that person has been created by God. If a Hebrew has been liberated from slavery, he (and later, or possibly from the very beginning, she) is a free person within a free community. Nobody has the right to sell or trade in people. It is interesting that the slave trade was tackled long ago within the Hebrew community. It was accepted as part of life in Roman and New Testament times and only seriously attacked in comparatively recent times by the European colonial powers. Attacking it was not a long jump from seeing the evil of depriving people of their freedom and of depriving those people of their property. Theft is an invasion of another person's life, and although the theft of the object itself may do minimum material damage, the invasion has been made and the community has been affronted. A sensitive approach is taken by Dante in his *Divine Comedy*. In *Inferno* (canto 25) he explores the effect of thievery on the thief himself. He depicts thieves as totally unstable in their bodily shapes, since they never know what is rightly theirs nor where the boundaries of their neighbors' property lie.

20:16   The ninth commandment is concerned with the giving of evidence falsely in public courts. It is not concerned with gossip and calumny uttered over the garden fence or in the tabloid press. The distinction is a rather fine one, especially when so much can be openly published that denigrates the character of public figures. Nevertheless, the situation addressed is that of Hebrew society, where village elders presided over village courts with a right of appeal to clan elders and eventually to the king. The whole complicated apparatus of modern Western law with its massive legal industry is not imagined in the commandment, though the principle remains. It is the right of all members of God's community to have the truth told about them in public, and to have an opportunity for self-defense. The case of Naboth is classic (1 Kings 21). He was convicted and put to death on false evidence. This can be extended to argue that any attempt to prevent the truth about a person from being told in public is an offense against that person, the community, and God. Thus imprisonment without trial, or without a proper open trial, is an offense against this commandment, since it effectively prevents the truth from being told. It perverts justice, since it leads the rest of the community to assume either that the prisoner must be guilty, or that because his cause is popular he must be innocent. God's community is one in which justice must be seen and heard in order to be done.

20:17   The tenth commandment, "You shall not covet," has often been emasculated. It has been interpreted as a general injunction against acquisitiveness. To begin with, the English word "covet" should be retained in translation. The word is obsolete and difficult to translate into other languages, but at least it does not give a false impression. The Hebrew verb occurs in other places in the Old Testament (Exod. 34:24; Josh. 7:21; Deut. 7:25; Mic. 2:2; Prov. 12:2; and Ps. 68:17) and has the general meaning of "hankering after" something, sometimes in a good sense, sometimes in a bad sense. Some interpreters have argued that many of the laws in the book of Deuteronomy are, in fact, applications of the tenth commandment. This suggestion has been taken further, so that coveting is equated with "depriving an elder of his status." In this case, an elder would presumably be the head of a family or clan. If this notion is right, then the story of Naboth (1 Kings 21) may enlighten the commandment. Merely by plotting to deprive Naboth of his vineyard, his stake in Israel, and therefore a possession he was unwilling to sell, even for a fair price, Jezebel broke this commandment. Each Israelite head of a family had a share in the Promised Land within the tribal inheritances. God's liberation and promises pointed materially to the land that, under God, was supposed to belong to all the families of Israel. This illuminates Isaiah's strictures against those "who join house to house" (Isa. 5:8). In the prophet's day, the amassing of property by the rich at the expense of the poor deprived some of the poorer families of their share in the land and of their rightful inheritance. It threatened the nature of the liberated community itself. "House" means household, not a building. The listing of various other people and animals, down to "anything that belongs to your neighbor," leaves no doubt about what is intended.

Far from being an ancient relic or a general piece of advice, the tenth commandment is a challenge to the greedy society of all ages. The gravy train, the embezzlement of public funds — anything that deprives the poor of resources is a form of covetousness and a perversion of the justice of God, however legally it may be done.

20:18-21 The Ten Commandments are set in the middle of a theophany. Yahweh appears in awe-inspiring power. *Then* the commandments are given. The first reaction is *fear*. The people appeal to Moses to place himself between them and Yahweh, for they are frightened to death of this new God. Moses turns this panicky fear into a different sort of fear, the fear of respect and obedience. The people are assured that Yahweh wants a live and bold pioneering people, not a cowering rabble of slaves.

Neither the Sermon on the Mount, nor indeed any of the teachings of Jesus, is intended to replace or subvert the Torah as delivered at Sinai. Indeed, the Sermon could almost be described as a *midrash,* an extended application, of the Sinai revelation, delivered with the authority of another Moses. The "freedom charter" intended for one specific people became a charter for the whole of human society and has changed the history of the whole human race.

THE ALTERNATIVE SOCIETY
Exodus 20:22–23:19

In many commentaries boredom seems to set in at this point, relieved only by the golden calf incident narrated in chapter 32. Comments on the text become brief. The impression is given that the writer of Exodus has now inserted into a brilliant narrative a series of rules and regulations that are of interest only to historians. This approach is thoroughly mistaken.

The Torah has been given by God at Sinai. It must now be applied to the living, continuing community in whatever situation it exists. Yahweh and Israel must relate to each other, not only in an initial, dazzling encounter, but in real life, which goes on. Religion is to be lived out, not left as a past experience. This conviction is integral to the biblical tradition. For Christians, it receives full expression in the incarnation of the Son of God. Authentic faith is a "faith for living."

The provisions of the latter chapters of the book of Exodus, concerning, say, the treatment of domestic animals or the structure of the tabernacle may seem pedestrian to twentieth-century Western people. Yet they were vital to Hebrew society for many centuries when the Pentateuch tradition was being formed. It is up to later generations to find out what the covenant laws mean and to apply their theological principles to their life situations. At the heart of all of them is relationship with God. The words "You are my people; I am your God" have to be applied to the continuing community of the Hebrews. This has to be done in two ways, as enunciated in the Ten Commandments. Relationship with Yahweh is expressed visibly in worship, that is, in sacrifices offered. Relationship between individuals and between households is expressed in social laws and customs. These two belong together as they do in the Ten Commandments. This has always been hard to grasp, especially in the modern Western world, where religion tends to be kept separate from social life and restricted to acts of public worship. Since these acts are attended by the few, many people see them as irrelevant to relationships in society at large. This attitude of making religion almost a private hobby for interested individuals contrasts strongly with the whole of biblical teaching. It also contrasts with the ancient cultures of Asia, Africa, and Latin America.

It is no wonder that the relationship proclaimed at Sinai must now be concretely expressed in the two great areas of life. Israel must be given clear instructions about what sacrifices to offer and about when, where, and by whom they should be offered. Any practice involving any other deity but Yahweh is to be excluded. Israel must also be given clear instructions about justice in all areas of community life. All of life is to be an act of worship, and every area of life should be brought into conformity with God's will since all of life is part of God's creation. Yahweh's sheer goodness and justice demand that (a) he be worshipped solely, persistently, and wholeheartedly and that (b) his character be lived out in the community of his people in goodness and justice towards each other. Coming from Sinai the Hebrews can never be the same. They are now a responsible people. The subsequent history of Israel is a continual application of Sinai. The Hebrew prophets confronted their contemporaries in the name of the God of Sinai. So, as the centuries went by, the lifestyle of the Hebrews developed from that of a mixed group of slaves to that of a settled, defined society.

Some of the regulations of the Pentateuch are seen today as being obsolete and even repugnant. They should rather be seen as stages in the ongoing process of distinguishing between God's demands, which are timeless, and human responses to those demands, which are imperfect and limited. Our response should certainly not be to reject what we see as outmoded, but to interpret the underlying demands of God more effectively to our own society.

The Torah legislation is not unique in every respect but shows many striking resemblances to the practices of neighboring ancient Near Eastern cultures. Much work has been done by archaeologists and Old Testament scholars on this subject (see James B. Pritchard, ed., *Ancient Near Eastern Texts Relating to the Old Testament,* 3rd ed., 159-98). Nevertheless, despite undeniable similarities in the treatment of criminals, in the settlement of civil disputes, in land tenure laws, in the treatment of slaves, in marriage customs, and in many other areas of life in community, there is a very significant difference in presentation. The Torah legislation is not presented as a code with the sanction of various gods behind it, but as the will of *one* God. Nor is it presented as the work of a sacral ruler or even of a statesman, despite the respect that is accorded to Moses. Nor is it presented as the wisdom of the sages. Rather, it is presented as the will of God himself for his people, resulting from a theophany, the revelation of Yahweh himself at Sinai. "I spoke with you from heaven" (Exod. 20:22).

The cultures of the ancient Near East were vastly different from modern Western culture. Canaan was dotted with small, cramped, walled towns. In the fields surrounding these towns, corn and vines were grown. The fields were marked off from each other by stones, not by fences or hedges; they were open to human and animal marauders. Domestic animals — sheep, cattle, donkeys — were used for food, transport, and labor. Goods were bought and sold by bargaining, or by weighing out loose metal (later by exchange of coins). Contracts were drawn up by scribes for marriages and for land. Disputes were settled by local elders. For long periods society was stable, and there were generally accepted standards of morality. Most people did not travel great distances, except for trade, in unsettled times of war, or when there was a drought.

The centralization both of government and of public worship was a slow and painful process. This was still going on even at the time when the book of Exodus received its final form. This means that the Pentateuch does not reflect a society cast in concrete, but a society struggling to adapt while struggling to be faithful to ancient tradition and to its God.

20:22-26   The ban on handmade images (20:4) is reinforced. Even the most expensive materials (such as gold) are totally inadequate to represent the God who "speaks from heaven."

100

Altars are physical places where connection is made between human beings and their gods, between the visible and invisible, the mundane and the sacred. Sacrifices are offered on them. It is vitally important that they should be appropriately constructed. Hebrew altars must not be replicas of Canaanite altars, lest they be tempted to worship Canaanite gods. They must not bear the marks of human fabrication, since that would be halfway to idolatry. Natural materials must be used such as earth or drystone, that is, uncut stone. There must be no hint of the Canaanites' sexual fertility cults.

These regulations imply that there were many crudely constructed altars up and down the land when the Hebrews first settled in Canaan. At these places Yahweh's power was liberated and available to bless his people as they offered sacrifices. Partly because people flouted the covenant and offered sacrifices at those altars to gods whom they thought would answer their requests, and partly because worship was centralized at the Jerusalem Temple, the reforms of King Josiah (seventh century BCE) banned the use of local altars (2 Kings 23). Stronger measures than these were eventually taken to prevent the worship of other gods. Apostasy was a very serious matter.

21:1-11   In the ancient Near Eastern world of the Old Testament period, it was normal for families to own slaves. They were property and belonged to their masters, who had purchased them legally. The right of purchase was respected, and the principle of slavery never challenged in the Bible, not even in the New Testament. Before writing off the biblical teaching as being strangely blind to an oppressive and abhorrent practice that our modern world has rejected, it is as well to register two qualifications. First, teaching about slaves needs to be examined so that its humanitarian concerns may be taken into account. Second, we should examine modern practices very carefully to see if slavery has in fact been eradicated in the spirit as well as in the letter. The Torah in Exodus about slaves is not concerned so much about the principle as about the practice. It is concerned with the rights of owners and with the humane treatment of people. Hence the length of service (six years) and the terms of service are designated. The terms of release of slaves are also indicated. Although slaves were considered property, they were also recognized as human beings with rights.

Slavery should not be seen in isolation from other forms of employment. Migrant labor, cheap labor, child labor, and other forms of labor can be just as exploitative as outright slavery and can give less hope of eventual release than the six-year tenure of Hebrew slaves. In contemporary situations, workers often have little option for improvement, and their conditions are not far removed from slavery. Indeed, they can be more oppressive. Thus the biblical insight of caring for both employer and employee has much to be said for it. Do employers in our day care for the needs and feelings of employees, and can those employees escape to other work and conditions? Do trade unions take into account the needs of employers or of the community as a whole? The instructions in Exodus 21 should not be written off merely because they accept slavery, but heeded as a very early attempt to apply God's justice to work relationships.

It was common practice in the Near East for female slaves to become wives or concubines (v. 7). Before condemning this right of the master to dispose of his female slave as he thinks fit, two points should be noted. First, he did have to provide her with food, clothing, and "marital rights" (which probably meant oil for cooking and lighting, rather than the modern connotation of sexual intercourse). Second, it was not so very long ago that the *jus primae noctis* (the right to have the first night) was a legal right for nobility in Europe (witness Beaumarchais's *Le Barbier de Seville*, echoed in Mozart's opera *The Marriage of Figaro*).

21:12-27   When violence takes over in relationships between people, what then? Violence shows no respect for the victim, who is also created by God. Therefore violence shows no respect of Yahweh himself. In ancient Near Eastern law codes, such as the code of Hammurabi, the severity of the penalty for violent acts typically depends on the social status of the victim. In the Torah, by contrast, there is no discrimination on the basis of social standing.

Murder, punishable by death, is clearly distinguished from

manslaughter, or culpable homicide (vv. 12-14). It is the *intention* that matters. Did the offender premeditate his attack? If he did not, then he could claim the protection of Yahweh by finding a sacred building and taking refuge at its altar.

21:15, 17   The fifth commandment, concerning respect for parents, is so important that even to strike or curse one's parent brings the death penalty.

21:16   This verse is a commentary on the eighth commandment, if that commandment originally referred to stealing of *people* rather than possessions. If a person is sold into slavery (as Joseph was), or kept under duress, then he has been treated as a nonperson. His rights and his person have not been respected. In our own century, whole races have been assigned to new rulers without their consent. We are not dealing with laws aimed at obsolete situations.

21:18-21   Slaves were admittedly seen as property in ancient Israel. Yet no other ancient Near Eastern laws lay down punishments for mistreating them. Certainly a long time elapsed before slaves were seen as people. It took even longer for the very institution of slavery to be attacked and abolished. These verses represent the beginning of a long process that culminated in the abolition of slavery. More important by far, here in the Torah legislation slaves begin to be taken into account in relationships within the community. Paul's letter to Philemon provides eloquent testimony, many centuries later than Exodus and in the Christian community, to the *novelty* of this idea. Slaves had to be seen as people, not merely as property, before they could be treated as people. Only then could any society tackle the institution. Events in South Africa have shown that the first step in tackling the institution of apartheid was to see every person as a person. Every person, whether white or black, whether employer or employee, whether educated or uneducated, had to be recognized as a person and treated as such. Only when this happened could the ideology be tackled and society changed. The abolition of apartheid not only in one country, but in all countries, is but another step in the implementation of the Torah. There is still a long, long way to go.

21:22-27   A miscarriage was a serious matter for the community, since it endangered the continuing life of the community. Children were at a premium. If the cause was violence from another man, then it was doubly serious, and the emotive and stern language of the so-called *lex talionis* ("an eye for an eye") is used. The principle of punishment fitting crime was not merely a primitive expression of revenge. It was a *limiting* principle. It was designed to *contain* damage and to *limit* blood feud. Far from being applicable to primitive or unstable societies where revenge was the normal reaction, it expresses the first step towards the Cross. First limit violent reprisals, then absorb all violence and revenge. If, for example, the *lex talionis* had been applied in Europe in 1914, Gavrilo Princip *alone* would have been executed for the murder of the Archduke Franz Ferdinand in Sarajevo. Instead of the wholesale carnage of the trenches in the First World War, instead of ethnic cleansing by murder or starvation in Rwanda and Bosnia in our own time, the principle of "an eye for an eye" would have limited the killing to one guilty person — not millions. Instead of innocent bystanders, those who perpetrated crimes would pay the price. Of course the *lex talionis* does not go so far as a refusal to return violence with violence. Yet it is a considerable advance on current practice in our supposedly civilized world. Once again there is discrimination, since the slave is treated differently. If he suffers violence from his master, he does not have the right to retaliate but is to be set free. Jesus' comment on "an eye for an eye" was "If anyone strikes you on the right cheek, turn the other also" (Matt. 5:39). In saying this he was not contradicting or even superseding Exod. 21:23-25, but opening up limitless horizons.

21:28–22:4   Dangerous domestic animals are the responsibility of their owners. Responsibility comes first, even to the point that storage pits must be adequately covered. After responsibility comes compensation for loss. Domestic animals were essential for the livelihood of the society for which these prescriptions were written. If they were lost, injured, or stolen while in someone else's care, responsibility had to be taken for them and compensation agreed upon. This was a community matter, not a private agreement. Yet if these animals turned vicious and attacked humans, then they were to be held accountable. They were to be stoned to death, and even their dead carcasses had to be rendered unfit for human consumption. Thus both owner and animals are held responsible. Thirty silver pieces, the compensation for the loss of a slave, echoes down biblical history. It is quoted as the price paid for the betrayal of Jesus (Matt. 27:9).

22:5-15   This legislation carries even further the principle of responsibility for actions, even if those actions have no malicious intent. A veld fire, started to burn off old grass and stimulate new growth, can get out of hand. It can be fanned by the wind and rage across neighboring land and burn up houses and threaten human life. Agriculture is not a private affair, but a community activity. What happens on one parcel of land may well affect others and, if damage results, then compensation has to be arranged. This has tremendous consequences, far beyond the burning of the grass. Actions undertaken by any enterprises are bound to affect the community as a whole, if not the *world community*. In our day this applies to disposing of noxious waste, overfishing the seas, building projects that encroach on the living space of people and animals, and a host of other activities. Commerce and industry should not be concerned purely with profits. Once again, the prescriptions of the Torah are not mere legal relics of obsolete agrarian societies but principles for human responsibility on a global scale.

22:16-31   In the "alternative society" of Israel, no distinction is made between religion and politics, or between response to Yahweh and respect for one's neighbor. This is why the basic law of the Ten Commandments appears to be applied haphazardly. Orders concerning the cult are mingled with the practical requirements of daily living. This is deliberate. It is just as important to get the relationship with God right as it is to get social justice right. Hence, prescriptions about the offering of sacrifices sometimes follow those concerned with social matters. Those whom

Yahweh has liberated from Egypt must respond to him by being responsible to him and to the society created by him.

Paternity is a moral responsibility, not just a biological consequence of sex. Casual sex and consequent one-parent families had no place in Hebrew society. This is emphatically not because of abstract principles of morality or because there was some sort of puritanical bias against sex. Sexual activity was not seen as a gift given to humans for them to indulge in carelessly. It was linked with human love and care, not only between the parties intimately concerned, but in society as a whole.

The bride price, *mōhar* in Hebrew society, *lobolo* in African society, has been scandalously misjudged as a financial transaction that treats girls as property to be bartered. In fact, these arrangements express family relationships and responsibilities to society as a whole. Hence a man who seduces a virgin must accept responsibility for his actions and pay an agreed price. This price must compensate for the damage he has done both to her and to her family. It is interesting that this principle — treating seduction as a matter for damages — stands in contrast to adultery, which involves a *married* woman. This distinction is still drawn in Xhosa society in rural Southern Africa. *Indleko* is paid when an unmarried girl is seduced, whereas adultery between married people is treated quite differently. Even allowing for the double standard at work in early Hebrew society, sexual affairs are treated here in the Torah as community matters related to the worship of Yahweh and to the well-being of the community as a whole. They are not matters of individual morality subject to the vagaries of public opinion or class attitudes.

22:18   This verse is cryptic. A witch or female sorcerer is, almost by definition, someone who manipulates unseen powers for personal ends and is usually paid to do so. This offends Yahweh, who alone controls such powers. It also offends the victims and the community at large. No wonder, then, that the death penalty is incurred.

22:19   This law regards bestiality (sex involving an animal) as offensive not because it is an abhorrent sexual practice. Rather, the law is aimed at some idolatrous Canaanite practices in which union with a god was achieved through sexual intercourse with the animal that was the god's physical representation.

22:20 Absolute loyalty to Yahweh is the first requirement of Sinai. All apostasy is banned (put under the *ḥerem*). This is the foundation of all life in the Hebrew community.

22:21 Of all the commands to care for others, the command to care for "aliens" is the most poignant. Whether these aliens were Hebrews living away from home or foreign immigrants, they were *vulnerable,* and vulnerable people are the special concern of Yahweh. After all, he has rescued vulnerable slaves from Egypt. He expects his people to care for the vulnerable people among them, no matter where they come from. The injunction that the Hebrews care for those people who were not their immediate responsibility yet lived among them reflects a much deeper and more profound principle. *All vulnerable people must be cared for.* In all human societies, foreigners are perceived as a threat, whether they speak a different language or not, whether their appearance is different or not, whether they come from far away or from the next village. The laws concerning aliens exclude all exploitation of migrants, all apartheid, all ethnic cleansing, all forced removals, all racial prejudice. These things are unworthy of God's people. It is true that the scale of the issue addressed by the biblical law is smaller than that of the modern world. The picture of Exod. 22:21 is of migrants attaching themselves to well-established Hebrew homesteads. All that is to be demanded of them is that they accept Yahweh as Lord and God. Yet this was a small beginning to a great movement aimed at the unity of the whole human race. Much later in Israelite history, the prophet Zechariah expected whole nations to attach themselves to the Hebrews in order to seek their God (Zech. 8:20-23). The book of Acts records a gradual and, it has to be admitted, hesitant acceptance of Gentile converts into the Christian community, which initially consisted of Jews. Yet in our day, foreigners, even in small numbers, stand little chance of being accepted and cared for in most countries. This is true even of countries with a

Christian heritage, and it is also true of countries that have the economic resources to cope with immigrants.

Within the Hebrew community, widows and orphans were liable to be neglected unless tied into family structures. They were the most vulnerable members of the community itself. During the period of the monarchy, the king was responsible for their care and protection, as indeed for that of all vulnerable and oppressed people (Ps. 72:1-4). Thus the leadership took over the responsibility of the community for its needy members. Yet the threat in verse 24 — "Your wives will become widows and your children orphans" — is uttered in order to bring home to the community as a whole that it must assume responsibility for its vulnerable members.

22:25 No interest is to be charged. Again, the aim is protection of the poor. No Israelite is to be reduced to a state of dependency or distress. Debt can reduce people to effective slavery, a far more grinding slavery than that of a legal slave, whose master is at least obliged to provide for him. In our own world, there are countless examples of people being oppressed by debts and many examples of whole nations being reduced to such a state. A combination of international financial pressure and local mismanagement has led to many underdeveloped nations being far more oppressed and ground down by their debts than they used to be under colonial rule. This is the very reason why usury (the charging of interest) is banned in the Torah. Given all the arguments in favor of this practice (compensation for the use of the lender's money, compensation for inflation, etc.), the wisdom of the prohibition has yet to be examined seriously. It may be that the charging of interest has created the financial problems it was intended to solve, or at least exacerbated them. The care implied in the prohibition is expressed in very practical terms. If a cloak or blanket is pawned, it must be returned before nightfall because the owner needs it to keep warm.

22:28 This prohibition is aimed at apostasy rather than merely at good manners. "Cursing" means repudiating, and to repudiate one's leaders and elders involves breaking the relationship with

Yahweh transmitted through succeeding generations. It is not angry insults that are at issue but a conscious rejection of God and the traditions of faith passed down within the community.

There is no theological difference between an offering and a sacrifice. Firstfruits — of humans, animals, and vegetables — were to be taken from every area of human life and offered to God by sacrifice. The whole system of sacrifice was a joyful and grateful acknowledgment that God had created a livable and bountiful life for his people. These sacrifices were a statement of faith expressed in practical and physical ways. But they also needed to relate to the needs of the community and to the very character of the Being to whom they were offered — Yahweh himself. Hence, in contrast to the customs of the Canaanites, the Hebrews never immolated human beings. If they ever did so, they were roundly condemned, since this constituted not only inhumanity but disobedience and apostasy. The slaughtering of domestic animals also had to be done in such a way that it did not impoverish the community; therefore, less valuable domestic animals were to be substituted for more valuable ones.

The prohibition against eating the carcass of an animal slaughtered by a wild beast reflects not simply an ancient taboo or a hygienic concern. The blood of a slaughtered animal belonged to Yahweh because blood symbolized the life belonging to the God who had created it. An animal killed by a wild beast would be an unfortunate accident, and its blood could not be offered by a community that had no intention of offering it. Such a carcass should be given to the domestic waste disposal agents — the dogs.

23:1-13 *Justice* is constitutive of the very person of Yahweh. It is not an abstract value or virtue. It is a revelation from God himself. God is just and righteous, and he therefore expects his people to be just and righteous. Therefore, faithfulness to Yahweh is the first step in justice. Hebrews who offer sacrifices at the shrines of other gods cannot be just, no matter what else they do. Likewise, the society they belong to cannot be just, since it is poisoned by their apostasy. Righteousness is first and foremost a theological property, not a natural or legal value.

Justice also demands respect for fellow human beings. Members of Yahweh's community had to learn that they could not combine assiduous and lavish worship of Yahweh with oppression of each other. These two sides of justice have never been resolved. Some Christians regard their personal faith in the Lord Jesus and their corporate worship as the most important marks of their Christianity. Other Christians regard caring for underprivileged human beings around them as their greatest Christian obligation. These two groups often despise each other. Yet both are needed if the community as a whole is to respond to Yahweh's demands and to the teaching of Jesus. This is why the minute demands of justice are intermingled with the minute demands of the cultus in the Pentateuch. This juxtaposition is also found in prophetic teaching. No clearer statement of the primacy of justice can be found in the Old Testament than Mic. 6:8, "What does the Lord require of you but to do justice and to love kindness (Hebrew *ḥesed*) and to walk humbly with your God?"

23:1-3   When justice has to be implemented in the courts, then impartiality has to be the guiding principle. These verses utter warnings against "following a majority," that is, being manipulated by the majority or by public opinion. The giving of untrue or malicious evidence is also condemned. The courts suffered and have always suffered from these and many other practices. God dispenses all justice, and it is up to his human agents to see to it that justice is done to all. This is just as relevant to the mighty legal industry of the Western world as it was to rural Israel.

23:4-5   Domestic animals are to be returned to their owners or be assisted to their feet if they have fallen down, even if they belong to a personal enemy or to an opponent at law.

23:6-8   The guiding principle in the practical application of justice is not equality before the law but love for fellow beings in the community. This is why concern for the poor and oppressed and underprivileged members of the community is a recurring theme in the Torah and throughout the Old Testament. Yahweh has chosen a poor and oppressed race. That race must, in turn, care for the poor and oppressed among them. The scales of justice must not be tipped in favor of those who have the advantage of being rich or privileged. What is more, the "poor" are not simply those who do not have a living wage. If that were the case, we could boast that, by the standards of biblical times and of the third world in our own times, the poor have been eliminated in the Western world. The biblical poor are all those at the bottom of the pile and those who are pushed around or ignored by the powerful. They are not the "criminal classes" either, but those who "walk humbly with their God." Putting together the qualities of poverty, meekness, humility, vulnerability, and faithfulness to God yields a more accurate picture of what the Bible usually means by "the poor."

23:10-19   The produce of the sabbatical (seventh) year belongs to the poor. Whether this law remained a dead letter, this provision for the less fortunate members of the community is a token of the concern demanded of the community. The sabbatical year echoes the Sabbath day. Both are *time* set apart for the celebration of Yahweh the Creator. Both are concerned with the needs of the community, with rest from labor for all and with food for all. So also with the other festivals. Most of the great yearly festivals had their origins in the work of the fields. Evidently, in Canaan the year originally began when the last of the harvest had been gathered, that is, in autumn. The work to prepare for a new year then began. This seems to have been superseded by a spring beginning to the year, when the new growth began to appear. The origins of the Hebrew festivals were rather complicated and remain uncertain. What is certain is that the festivals were related to agriculture, not to an arbitrary calendar, and that they were subordinated to theological considerations: (1) The festivals celebrate Yahweh alone. No other gods of corn, wine, or weather are to be worshipped. (2) The festivals involve all God's people, rich and poor alike. The poor especially must be included by ensuring that they have a reason to celebrate. (3) The festivals are no longer seasonal events alone and do not promote worship of sun, moon, and stars. They now commemorate the mighty acts of God in history, including the liberating Exodus from Egypt.

Strange to say, the laws in this part of Exodus make no provisions for the celebrating of Passover, although there is a possible allusion to it in verse 18. Indeed, there are very few references to the feast before the account of its revival under King Josiah (2 Kgs. 23:21-23). The Passover may not have been observed until the Deuteronomic revival under Josiah. Possibly, only a spring feast of unleavened bread was held. This would have involved more than a cereal feast, since all feasts worth holding would have included a *zebah,* a meal of meat from a sacrificed animal. It may have taken some time for the great historical events of Israel's past to be conflated with the agricultural feasts of the year in Canaan. The great reformer Josiah rediscovered Passover as ideally suited to take the conscience of the Hebrew nation back to its origins. The very character of the Passover liturgy, nomadic and celebrated in family groups, was well-suited to bringing the people back to their origins. Later still, Ezra found it to be the ideal feast for marking a new act of liberation by Yahweh, the return from exile in Babylon. Jesus completed the chain of historical events by his death at Passover and by his commandment that his followers perpetuate the feast.

The instruction, "You shall not boil a kid in its mother's milk" (v. 19), has nothing to do with hygiene or with animal rights. It was probably aimed at a Canaanite practice. If the verse is a warning against some form of apostasy (and it is difficult to see how it could refer to anything else), then the vexed question of syncretism is raised. Syncretism, the mixing of elements of one religion with another, is never condemned outright in the Old Testament. There is plenty of evidence that the Hebrews were profoundly influenced by the practices and the thought world of the ancient Near East. This does not seem to have worried any of the Old Testament writers. They were more concerned with whether those practices promoted or compromised total allegiance to Yahweh alone. If any practice led to apostasy, to any weakening of the I-Thou relationship between Israel and her God, then that practice had to be rejected. Many modern Christians and Jews abhor syncretism and scrupulously avoid any contact with other religions. Even Christmas day falls under the suspicion of some because it may have begun as a "pagan" feast. This is not a biblical attitude. Not all practices adapted from other cultures or religions are attacked in Scripture, but only those that reject, ignore, or undermine the people's relationship with the one true God. The proscription against boiling a baby goat may well be a garbled piece of irrelevance, but the difference between syncretism and apostasy should give pause to a culture that is tolerant of every form of magic and that has forgotten the mighty acts of God.

THE COVENANT RATIFIED
Exodus 23:20–24:18

The Ten Words have been spoken, and the first set of covenant laws has been given. Now follows a promise of the conquest of Canaan and a ceremony of covenant ratification. The Hebrews must now bind themselves and their descendants to their protector and God. They do this by enacting the most solemn ritual known to them, the covenant of blood. When, in later times, the Hebrew prophets reminded Israel of her relationship to Yahweh, they referred to this event. It was a relationship accepted once for all under Moses, negotiated face-to-face at the holy mountain and sealed in blood. The scene of covenant ratification described in 23:3-8 has a revelatory counterpart in 23:1-2, 9-11. These verses describe Moses and the leaders of Israel ascending the mountain to see God and to share a meal. Thus, Torah, sacrifice, and theophany meet together in this section.

23:20-33   The Hebrews will enter the Promised Land and will settle there. God will continue to sponsor and protect them, but the people must obey and not rebel against an angel that Yahweh will send ahead of them to guide them to Canaan. This angel with Yahweh's name in him is a sort of verbal insulator separating the utter majesty of Yahweh from his frail people. The language used to describe the angel means "God at one remove." The Hebrew word *mal'ak* and its Greek translation *angelos* both mean "messenger." The words do not carry with them imagery of golden beings with sweeping wings, but of God delivering his own word in person, as his own messenger. The message is that God will protect Israel. Indeed, he will dwell *in* Israel.

In practical terms, Yahweh will deal with invaders and

marauders and with the inhabitants of Canaan. The weapons of terror and pestilence (or "hornets"; the meaning of the Hebrew is unclear) recall the plagues used against Egypt. They do not belong to the Hebrews, and the Hebrews have no control over them. In return, there is to be no apostasy, no worship given to any other gods, no lapsing into the cults of neighboring peoples, but only absolute loyalty to Yahweh alone. In return for this, the continuation of life is guaranteed. "None shall cast her young or be barren in your land" (v. 26).

This passage, along with similar passages dealing with holy war, has caused much concern. Taken together, the biblical texts describing holy war have been used to provide a theological justification for waging a "just war." The language of these passages is undeniably warlike. Nevertheless, the war theme has to be seen in the context of the Bible as a whole. It cannot be isolated from the full range of biblical teaching and used to legitimize this or that war. War is the responsibility of those who wage it. Taking up arms against oppressors, dictators, evil systems, and racist or sectarian regimes has a certain legitimacy. Yet the victory of the "God of battles" is not the routing of Canaanites but the kingdom of God fully expressed in the life of the people of God.

More immediately, the goal of Yahweh's campaign for Israel as described in the Pentateuch and the historical books is not the military defeat of the enemy, but total submission to Yahweh. The ultimate aim is not a victorious occupation of Canaan. The campaign continues, and its nature changes. It becomes a battle for the soul of Israel. Does Israel really belong to God? Will Israel respond to God's love? Is Israel willing to become God's servant and to suffer to the death (Isaiah 40–55)?

The inhabitants of Canaan are to be driven out and no accommodation is to be made with them. On the surface this sounds very much like apartheid, which was the official policy of the South African government until the 1990s. Apartheid was a religious policy, justified by Christian theologians with appeals to such texts as Exod. 23:32-33. In fact, these instructions to Israel to keep herself separate have nothing to do with racial or political exclusiveness, let alone with color of skin. They are rather concerned with the exclusive devotion of Israel to Yahweh. Devout

Yahwists in ancient Israel perceived Canaanite religion as a threat to that devotion, especially in Elijah's time, when Canaanite Baal worship all but supplanted that of Yahweh.

In any case, Israel did not drive out all the previous inhabitants of Canaan. The language of Yahweh's victorious advance is not the language of an ethnic cleansing that never happened. It is the language of Yahweh claiming his people and the land he gave them to be devoted to the sole worship of the God who created it and them.

24:1-2, 9-11   Yahweh shows himself to the Hebrews, but only to seventy-four of them. These are the priestly leaders and elders, and the bulk of the people have to take their word for what they have seen. This pattern of revelation to a chosen few continues throughout Scripture. Moses alone witnesses the burning bush. Elijah alone hears the "still, small voice." Isaiah alone sees the vision in the Temple. So also with Jeremiah and Ezekiel. Jesus takes three disciples alone to see his transfiguration. Theophanies are not great media events.

The seventy elders are referred to again in Num. 11:24, where they are endowed with the Spirit of Yahweh. They may be the same elders chosen by Moses on Jethro's advice (Exod. 18:13-27), and their names are representative of all Israelites. The party goes up the mountain away from the rest of the people. On that mountaintop, a world apart, there is a sense of awe and majesty. The men are exposed to Yahweh. They see the God of Israel. The verbs of the senses (seeing, hearing, feeling) convey closeness to Yahweh, experiencing him, being in direct contact with him. This is borne out by what happens next. Yahweh appears to them sitting in glory and majesty as king and judge. His feet rest on a blue surface of some kind. English translations have been unable to find the right word to describe the surface. "Dais," "platform," and "pavement" seem too mundane; "firmament" sounds archaic. Perhaps the blue surface represents the solid dome over the earth described in Gen. 1:6-8 (cf. Ezek. 1:26-28) and conveys the idea that God presides over his whole creation. Moses and the leaders are granted the extraordinary privilege of being allowed a glimpse of God. Amazingly, they survive this experience unharmed. They eat and drink, evidently sharing in a kind of covenant meal (cf. Exod. 18:12, where Moses, Aaron, and the elders eat bread with Jethro "in the presence of God"). Amazement that anyone could see God and survive is reflected in the ancient translations. The Septuagint says that they saw *the place* where God stays and that they *were seen* there. Symmachus's version says that they saw the God of Israel *in a vision*. This daring assertion that mortal humans actually saw God signals both the beginning of a deeper understanding of God and a striking authentication of the Sinai event.

24:3-8   Enveloped in the description of the vision of God is the covenant sacrifice. First Moses writes the words of the Lord in a book or scroll, a detail that may be an anachronism (v. 7). The spoken word is being made physical and permanent. It is, in modern terms, being "set in concrete." Then it is sealed in sacrifice, involving the shedding of blood. An altar is built. Twelve cairns or pillars of stones are set up, representing the tribes, that is, the whole of Israel. "Young men" then slaughter the oxen. (These men are not priests or Levites, since this happens before the Aaronic priesthood, but able-bodied men of military age, acting on behalf of Israel.) This is a very important sacrifice. The largest and costliest domestic animals are used and totally given over to Yahweh as holocausts, total burnt offerings in which nothing is eaten by the offerers. Offerings of well-being are also presented. These are shared with the people and signal a solemn and joyful festival, a celebration. The word for "well-being," *šĕlāmîm*, is probably not connected with the well-known word *shalom*, "peace," but refers, in contrast with the whole offering, to a shared, celebratory sacrifice. One element was certainly not shared and that was the blood. This was drained off and then poured out for God. The pouring out of the blood is the most solemn binding part of the whole covenant. A covenant is not ratified by signing on a dotted line but by the blood of sacrifice. Thus the seal is set forever upon God's choice of Israel and Israel's acceptance of God.

The New Testament engages in a deliberate repetition of Sinai in its essentials. The transfiguration of Jesus reveals him to be the very glory of God. Then he is raised from the dead and ascends to glory and in glory. He gives the Torah. In fact he *is* Torah, the very embodiment of the commandments. At the Last Supper, he points to the definitive sacrifice he is to offer. The Cross is the new covenant in blood, because Jesus, the giver of the sacrifice, is also the covenant sacrifice. Every celebration of the Last Supper is a renewal and reapplication of that covenant sacrifice offered once and for all. The epistle to the Hebrews, chapters 8 and 9 especially, states clearly that Jesus' sacrifice on the Cross is the covenant sacrifice, only this time including all of humanity within its range.

The blood is collected in bowls and sprinkled over the book and over the Hebrews themselves. As the red blood stains their clothes, they share in the holiness of Yahweh. Their leaders have *seen* him; now they *feel* his holiness upon their very clothing and faces. No wonder that they reply, "All that the Lord has spoken we will do." They are now partners with the mighty God, bound together to him *forever*.

24:12-18   Moses again climbs the mountain and is again allowed to enter the glory. He is accompanied by Joshua, who also sees the glory and is thereby prepared for the next stage of leading Israel into the Promised Land. In similar fashion, when Peter, James, and John (Luke 9:28) see Jesus transfigured in glory, they are being prepared to lead the advance of the gospel into the whole world. Moses' second entry into the vision of the glory of Yahweh signals that the covenant is complete for Israel.

WORSHIP
Exodus 25:1–31:18

The experience of Sinai was never repeated, but the relationship between Yahweh and his people established at Sinai continued down through the generations. This relationship was expressed in a system of worship with sacrifice at its center. Ancient Israel's sacrificial system represented the people's continued devotion to Yahweh. It was therefore essential to "get it right" down to the last detail. Far from being a wearisome set of petty rubrics drawn up by some liturgist, these chapters in Exodus (25–31) present the score of a glorious symphony of sacrifice offered to the mighty God. The chapters present a series of detailed instructions, delivered to Moses by God, for the construction of the ark of the covenant, the tabernacle and its furniture, as well as priestly matters and daily sacrifices. The execution of these instructions is described later in chapters 35–40.

The material relating to the tabernacle can be confusing at times. Some passages in Exodus describe a mobile shrine (the "tent of meeting"; Exod. 33:7-11; cf. Num. 11:16-30; 12:4-10), while others picture a more substantial complex ("the tabernacle"; Exodus 25–27). Because the tent of meeting is the simpler structure, many scholars think that it reflects a more ancient tradition. The traditions concerning the tabernacle seem to be based on the later Jerusalem Temple built by Solomon in the tenth century BCE, long after the time of Moses. The traditions concerning the tent and tabernacle have apparently been combined in Exodus 25–27 to form "the tabernacle of the tent of meeting," so that the tent has become a covering for the tabernacle.

The influence of Solomon's Temple on the description of the tabernacle represents more than just an anachronism. It demonstrates the continuity of Hebrew worship down the ages and its unity with the original community of Sinai. The Christian Eucharist provides something of a parallel. The celebration of the Lord's Supper by any contemporary Christian community *cannot* be an exact replay of the original Supper at Jerusalem on the night before Jesus died. Yet, however different it may seem from what took place in the upper room, it is a continuity of the one act of worship commanded by Jesus himself.

In the Torah, the ordering of worship in all its details is just as important as the regulating of the day-to-day life of the community. The great symphony of sacrifices that developed down the ages responded to the first demand of Yahweh. The Hebrews must worship Yahweh alone, excluding all other deities or objects of worship. The sacrificial system is a *statement of faith,* a credo.

The making of the tabernacle deliberately reflects the creation of the world. Moses approves the completed work (Exodus 39–40) just as God had approved his creation (Genesis 1). The perfect ordering of worship reflects the perfect order of God the Creator. The arrangements of the tent and tabernacle for worship reflect God's plans for cosmic salvation.

Yahweh commits himself to dwelling among his people and meeting them at the tabernacle. This is a theological statement, typical of Judaism and Christianity. God leaves isolation and consents to dwell in a contraption made from the skins of animals and, later on, in an edifice constructed from stone. Yet he cannot be localized or tied down in any way. The God who is distinct from and immeasurably beyond his people is yet among them.

In the New Testament, the writer of the epistle to the Hebrews makes the claim that Jesus has fulfilled, in himself, all the demands of worship. He is the tabernacle, the high priest, and the sacrifice. In making this claim, the author of Hebrews is not dismissing tabernacle, priesthood, and sacrifice as outmoded mistakes but asserting that their purpose has been fulfilled. The symphony of sacrifice has reached its finale in the death of Jesus. Similarly, when the prologue to the Gospel of John proclaims that the Word became flesh and "tabernacled among us" (John 1:14), it is affirming that the incarnation of Christ is God's definitive drawing near to dwell with humanity.

When Jesus cleansed the Temple at Jerusalem (Mark 11:15-19 and parallels), he made a theological statement that was by no means unexpected in the Hebrew tradition. The prophet Ezekiel, to take but one example, had condemned the apostasy practiced in the first Temple and had a vision of the new temple for the ideal future (Ezekiel 40–48). Jesus drove out the animals and sent the coins rolling across the floor in order to show that Yahweh's instructions for the tabernacle were being flagrantly disobeyed. He was symbolically protesting that the Temple was not being properly treated as the place where God dwelt, where he met his people, and where they offered sacrifice. In the Gospel of John, Jesus claims to be able to raise up the destroyed Temple after three days, and the evangelist relates this to the death and resurrection of Christ: "But he spoke of the temple of his body" (John 2:19-21; cf. Mark 14:58).

25:1-9   The people themselves contribute the materials for the sanctuary (cf. 35:4-29): precious metals (gold, silver, and bronze); dyed yarns of linen; animal skins; and gem stones. All these were well-known in the ancient Near East, though they would have been costly and not readily obtainable at Sinai or in Canaan. The God of the Hebrews accompanies them as they travel, in a tent provided by them from materials that they have skillfully worked themselves.

25:10-22   The ark (Hebrew *'ărôn*) was a chest or large box, $45'' \times 27'' \times 27''$, made from acacia wood (cf. 37:1-9). It was carried about apart from the tabernacle at times and even taken into battle as a sort of sacred mascot or palladium (1 Samuel 4). Eventually, it was placed in the Jerusalem Temple by Solomon (1 Kings 8). After this, there is no record of what happened to it. Yahweh met and spoke with Moses at the ark (v. 22). It contained the "testimony," the slates of the Ten Commandments, the tangible witness of God's great communication with Israel. It was also regarded as the footstool of Yahweh's invisible throne (cf. 1 Chron. 28:2; Pss. 99:1; 132:7) and therefore as the focal point of his invisible presence with the people. Over the top of the ark was the *kappōret* (v. 17), the lid or "mercy seat." This word was translated into Greek as *hilastērion*, "propitiatory," the place where sacrifice was offered to reconcile Israel to her God (cf. Rom. 3:25). Sacrificial blood was sprinkled onto it by the high priest once in the year, on the Day of Atonement (Hebrew *yôm kippur*). The cognate verb, *kāpar*, means "to cover," and the intensive form of the verb, *kipper*, means "to obliterate, bury, cover up," often with reference to the removal of sin by means of sacrifice. Thus on the lid or covering of the chest that contained God's definitive words to Israel, Israel met her God in sacrifice, and all her sin and alienation and neglect were obliterated.

On either side of the *kappōret* are the *kĕrûbîm*, winged bulls or lions with human heads. Reliefs and statues of these sphinxlike creatures, in the role of guardians of temples, palaces, and other sacred buildings, have been found at various ancient Near Eastern sites. In the Old Testament they function to emphasize the transcendent holiness and majesty of Yahweh (cf. Gen. 3:24; 2 Sam. 22:11; 1 Kgs. 6:29; Ps. 18:10; Ezek. 41:18-19; etc.). They never came under the prohibition of images, presumably because worship was never offered to them.

There is paradox in the faith of the Hebrews. The God who bans all images of himself, let alone those of any other god, is to be met in sacrifice offered over the lid of a chest that has the figures of human-faced beasts at either end of it. The God who has never been seen at any time sends his Son, who tells his disciples, "If you have seen me, you have seen the Father" (John 14:9).

25:23-30 A table is to be placed for the "bread of the Presence" (cf. 37:10-16). This was not seen as Yahweh's daily ration of food but as a permanent vegetable sacrifice offered out of gratitude for the land and its produce.

25:31-40 The gold-plated lampstand *(mĕnôrâ)* was a permanent symbol of the light of God (cf. 37:17-24). It consisted of a single shaft on a tripod base. At the top of this shaft were six branches, and on top of each branch and the central stem were seven golden flowers. The lamps placed on these seven metal flowers were small bowls or jugs, each with seven spouts pierced in the lid. The number seven corresponds with the seven-day week and with the creation account of Genesis 1. The whole of life created by God is contained in this number, which represents theological, not mathematical, perfection. The lamps were filled with oil and kept lit at all times.

26:1-36   A whole chapter is devoted to the construction of the tabernacle. The architectural division of the tabernacle into inner and outer sanctums reflects the design of Solomon's Temple (1 Kings 6). So do the materials, such as the fine white linen and the blue, scarlet, and purple dyes, which belong more naturally to later periods of trade with Egypt and Phoenicia. Yet the animal skins (v. 14) could well belong to a nomadic life style.

Yahweh dwells among his people, whether they are sojourning in the desert or settled in the Promised Land. Yet, as the prophets insisted (e.g., Jer. 7:4), neither tabernacle nor temple replaced Yahweh as security for his people. They were Yahweh's "local domicile" *(miškān),* symbolizing his commitment to be among his people and to communicate with them.

The whole tabernacle complex was a kind of tent within a tent. It was portable. Wherever they went, the people of God carted Yahweh's dwelling around with them. It was the only permanent visible sign of their identity. It must have looked rather like a marquee or circus tent, with forty-eight frames and ninety-six bases. When erected and linked up by its rings and cross bars, the wooden framework would have taken up an area measuring $45' \times 15' \times 15'$. It had ten curtains of richly embroidered material and, like a bedouin tent, was open at one end. Over the tabernacle proper went a covering of goat hair, and over that went a sort of huge tarpaulin made from the skins of rams tanned red. This must have looked like a red leather sheath. The interior of the tabernacle, surrounded by a court, was divided into two sections by another embroidered curtain. The inner, smaller section was the "holy of holies" or "most holy place," which housed the ark. The outer, larger section, "the holy place," housed the table for the bread offering and the lampstand.

All this would have been a very ungainly pile of baggage to be transported across difficult terrain, and the description may well be a conflation of various accounts from various periods. Nevertheless, the attention devoted to the tabernacle in the narrative is intended to show that the relationship between the Hebrews and their God was expressed in a well-ordered cult of sacrifice from Sinai onwards. The description of the tabernacle also reflects the unity of the one tradition of worship from its nomadic origins to its fuller expression in the Jerusalem Temple.

27:1-8 The whole tabernacle functioned as a "macro altar" devoted to the offering of sacrifice. The main altar, upon which most of the animal sacrifices were offered, stood outside the holy place described above. Though referred to elsewhere as "the bronze altar," it was originally made of acacia wood, was hollow, and was overlaid with copper. The description in this chapter is a reconciliation of a wooden altar, light enough to be carried on trek, and the solid bronze altar fixed permanently in the Temple. This had a wood fire underneath it and a grill on top. The horn-shaped corners of the altar were used for smearing blood and for claiming the right of sanctuary (cf. Exod. 21:13). The theological significance of this account of the main altar of sacrifice is that *all* sacrifices must be offered to the *one* God on *one and the same* altar throughout the life of Israel.

27:9-19 Around the tabernacle was a court, open to the sky and fenced in by a linen screen that hung between 100 pillars with bronze bases. The entrance to this area was on the east side, concealed by a screen.

27:20-21 The priests are entrusted with the task of keeping the lamps lit with pure olive oil. This continually burning light served as a sign of God's presence and linked the succeeding generations of Hebrews.

28:1-43 The vestments of Aaron and of the other priests of his clan are prescribed in detail. Whatever authority and status Aaron had, there was no monarchic high priest in early Israel. The priestly office became more vital to the life of Israel once the monarchy ended and the Temple was rebuilt. The dress of the priests, like the ornaments of the tabernacle, reflected the glory, beauty, and holiness of Yahweh. In the Exodus prescriptions, this is transferred back to the original priest, Aaron, the brother of Moses. The priesthood was not an exclusive elite foisted on to Israel, but a living reflection of the honor due to Yahweh.

The ephod (28:6-14) was a vestment, a sort of kilt with shoulder straps. The "breastpiece" (28:15-30) was a sort of waist-coat with pouches for the Urim and Thummim. The etymology of these words remains uncertain, but they have been interpreted to mean "lights" and "perfections." They were twelve semipre-cious stones thrown down in order to seek a tangible opinion from Yahweh (cf. 1 Sam. 14:18). The practice of throwing down objects for purposes of divination was common in the ancient Near East, and similar practices continue in various contemporary cultures. Israel saw this not as a lottery but as an exercise of total trust in Yahweh. The early Christian Church drew lots to elect a disciple to replace Judas Iscariot (Acts 1:26).

Over these garments went a sleeveless robe (28:31-35), which was hung with alternate golden balls (pomegranates) and bells. Their tinkling as the high priest moved around either reminded him of the solemnity and danger of his task, or simply gave the alarm if they stopped ringing when he was hidden from sight in the holy of holies. The turban (28:36-39), which had on it a gold disc engraved with the words "holy to the Lord," may be derived from the diadem or tiara worn by the kings of Judah.

The priesthood (28:40-43) was hereditary in Israel. The offer-ing of sacrifices to Yahweh was so important that a special order of full-time officers was set apart and specially dressed solely to carry out those liturgies.

29:1-46   The ceremony of consecrating priests was not a certi-fication, since all able-bodied male descendants of Aaron were automatically priests by virtue of their birth. From that day on-ward, their life was set apart for the orchestration of the symphony of sacrifices that devoted the life of Israel to Yahweh. Sacrifices are to be offered in the service for ordination: cereal offerings with oil followed by valuable domestic animals — a bullock and two rams in mint condition (vv. 1-3). Then the priests wash themselves as a purification (v. 4) and put on the various garments (vv. 5-6). Holy oil is generously poured upon their heads (v. 7; cf. Ps. 133:2). The verb translated "ordain" in v. 9 is literally "to fill the hand of" and possibly relates to the priests being given their share of the sacrificial meat.

Before he offers life to the living God, the priest must be completely reconciled to Yahweh. He must be protected by the blood of the whole offering smeared on the horns of the altar and poured at its base. One of the rams is then sacrificed as an act of homage and celebration (vv. 15-18). The other ram is a shared offering, to be feasted on by the priests alone (vv. 19-28, 31-34). It is misleading to call this a "wave offering," as if a priest were waving the carcass of a ram in the air. Rather, the sacrifice was brought to the altar and then taken away again, to dramatize its presentation to God and then its reception by the priests (cf. NRSV: "elevation offering"). As a protection in the presence of the holy God, the blood of the sacrifice is smeared on the right side of the priests' bodies, on their right ears, right hands, and right feet. Through this blood, the priest becomes part of the movement of sacrifice.

The "sin offerings" deal with reconciliation, with cleaning away all obstacles in the relationship between Israel and Yahweh. They ensure that worship in the form of sacrifice was offered by a community that was in all respects right with its God. It was later the task of the prophets to teach Israel that being right with God involved both pure worship and pure community life. The Day of Atonement later came to express the tremendous need of Israel for reconciliation.

Yahweh's glory will make the tabernacle and its officers special and holy (v. 43). The experience of worship is glory. Corporate worship does provide windows for glory. It is not just a matter of carrying out duties. Through their worship, their offering of sacrifice by their own sanctified priesthood, the Hebrews are to *know*, that is *experience*, the past activity and present reality of their God.

30:1-10 The "altar" of incense was a brazier on top of which certain substances were burnt in a pan. The Hebrew word used

in 30:1, *(qĕṭōret),* refers to the smoke produced rather than to
the incense itself, which is one of the ingredients prescribed in
verses 30-34. The offering of a sweet-smelling smoke to a deity
is an ancient and still widespread custom. The objection to it in
some quarters of Christianity is hard to understand. Animals and
cereals were offered as precious gifts, and pleasing smoke was
seen as a tribute to the god. It came to signify prayer rising to
the Almighty. In the book of Revelation, whole bowls of incense
producing clouds of sweet smoke rise up as they represent the
prayers of the saints giving glory to the Lamb (Rev. 5:8; 8:3).

30:11-16   Contributing money (by weight or in coinage)
belongs to a settled lifestyle rather than to a desert existence. It
goes with the sacrifices for sin, whose purpose was to reconcile
the people to Yahweh and to ask for protection against his punishments, especially against plagues. By New Testament times, the
tax described here was levied for the upkeep of the Temple. Jesus
did not refuse to pay it but ordered it to be plucked from a fish's
mouth, to show that the Lord of the Temple was paying tax with
a contribution from creation itself (Matt. 17:24-27).

30:22-23   The recipe given here for the fragrant oil includes
substances extracted from plants. They must have been rather
expensive imports. The oil must have been used generously, since
at the consecration of Aaron it poured down from his beard to
the skirts of his robe (cf. Ps. 133:2). The chrism still used in many
Christian churches for confirmations and ordinations stands in
the same tradition. The anointing of Jesus' feet by the woman
(Mark 14:3; John 12:3) may have been a recognition of Jesus'
kingship and priesthood as well as an anointing of his body before
his burial. When Jesus dismissed Judas's objection to the woman's
action on the grounds of expense, he was drawing the attention
of those present to his own role as priest and king about to offer
himself as sacrifice.

31:1-11   God the Creator's own power enables the craftsmen
to construct a creation within which the Creator is fittingly worshipped. These verses are a blessing on all works of religious art

127

designed for the context of worship, whether buildings or vestments or works of art.

31:12-17   The Sabbath day, kept solemnly every week, is the sign and sacrament of Israel's allegiance to the one God, the Creator. It is a setting aside of time and a perpetual link between the present moment and creation as demanded by God himself at Sinai.

The Sabbath is called a "sign" (Hebrew *'ôt*), a word used both of acts of God (e.g., Exod. 4:8-9) and of significant events in Yahweh's dealings with Israel (e.g., Exod. 3:12; Josh. 4:6). It is to be a "perpetual covenant," a phrase used sparingly. Thus the weekly celebration of the Sabbath regularly brings the covenant into the present time. It is also a celebration, a blessed and happy day, not a niggardly day hedged about with prohibitions.

31:18   All of these instructions about the tabernacle and the worship offered in it are "written with the finger of God." This is not a crudely literal expression. Yahweh himself and no human being or liturgical committee has authorized the whole symphony of sacrifice in every detail as the covenanted communication between the Hebrews and their God. This verse also makes an implied contrast between the authentic worship of Yahweh and what is described in the next chapter — the golden calf.

THE COVENANT BROKEN
AND RENEWED
Exodus 32:1–34:35

The narrative of the golden calf incident is not merely an account of the wickedness of one people (the Hebrews) on one occasion (many years ago) at one place (Sinai). It is the story of the fall of the whole human race. It states the alternatives: *either* the covenant with the one God *or* the golden calf, a do-it-yourself god or gods. As such, the story of the golden calf is a fifth story of the Fall, parallel to the stories in Genesis 3–11. These stories do not simply record historical or primeval events, but contemporary accounts and assessments of the human race. In the account here in Exodus, God has chosen the Hebrews and they have accepted him. They then immediately, with indecent haste, flout him and disobey him. Instead of worshipping "I Am," they worship a calf that they themselves have fabricated out of stolen, or at least expropriated, Egyptian gold. Yet through this very rebellion they learn reconciliation, and they grow in spirit.

The sequence of events is typical of the way the Hebrews rebelled against Yahweh and of the way human beings rebel against their Creator. First, they grumble and complain. They do not trust Yahweh, despite what he has done for them already. They reject both him and their (temporarily) absent leader. With Yahweh discarded, they look for something tangible and malleable to worship. They rationalize this by telling themselves that they are not replacing him but representing him by an object that they can see. They replace "I Am" with the image of a young bull, an image used by other peoples of the ancient Near East, thereby violating the second of the Ten Commandments. The irony of the situation is endless. They intend to offer sacrifice to a caricature of a god in a caricature of a tabernacle. They reduce to a calf or young bull the God who conquered Pharaoh and all the gods of Egypt, who turned the Nile god into a bloody sacrifice. To celebrate this feat, the Hebrews hold a carnival and indulge in "revelry," a word that implies something far more riotous than a tea party. Thinking they have tamed God, the Hebrews relax their morals as well as their faith and proceed to hold an orgy.

In doing all this, the Hebrews have shattered the covenant. They have utterly betrayed Yahweh and broken their relationship with him. Moses smashes the tablets, not simply to register his anger but to demonstrate what they have done. Aaron cringes, pretends, and tries to lie his way out of the ordeal. The people have committed the ultimate in sin. The result is punishment, which is not the revenge of a jilted god but an object lesson in the consequences of idolatry.

The golden calf sort of god — the do-it-yourself god — is mercilessly lampooned in Isaiah 44 and other passages that condemn *all* idolatry. Whenever a creature, an ideology, or a human achievement is worshipped in place of God, then not only is God rejected but the demonic is released. No wonder the Hebrews were in uproar.

The very purpose of telling the story of the golden calf immediately after the giving of the Torah on Mount Sinai is to show that there never was a golden age without a golden calf, when the hearts of humans were pure. There never has been any such animal as Rousseau's noble savage. Despite this fact of life, God does not give up on his chosen people, but forgives them and shows them mercy. Both in Psalm 106 (vv. 20-21) and in Stephen's speech (Acts 7:39-43), the golden calf is the quintessential symbol of rebellion against God. It represents a turning back to Egypt for security, a return to abject slavery and to the worship of human creation. The Hebrews have a choice. They can either respond to God and the worship of him alone, or they can make golden calves. If they do the latter, then they will create their own gods and will become completely self-directed. That dead end leads to death.

32:1-5   The people have placed their trust in Moses, but Moses is absent. So they go to Aaron and ask him to "produce" God, as Moses had done. Whether to court popularity or to supplant Moses, Aaron complies. He produces a popular, well-known substitute for Yahweh. The golden calf, or young bull, is part of the immediate past for the Hebrews. It is crafted from Egyptian gold and is reminiscent of Apis, the Egyptian bull god. It also has Canaanite connections and looks to the future from the vantage point of Sinai. Why not use the bull image of the Canaanite baals in order to worship Yahweh through it? King Jeroboam I later adopted this policy when he led the northern tribes to break away from the united kingdom established by David and Solomon (1 Kings 12). Jeroboam's motives were political. By creating more places for worship of Yahweh, he intended to keep his new subjects away from Jerusalem and from the legitimate monarchy of the Davidic line. Jeroboam himself had been an exile in Egypt, having fled there from Solomon. There are so many strands to the story of the golden calf, both in Hebrew history and in human nature, that its message is inexhaustible. Every time racial purity or national identity or self- or group-interest is clothed with a religious sanction, then the golden calf is remade. A god is then reborn, a god made by human beings for human beings, a do-it-yourself god, an idol.

32:6 The verb translated "play, revel," *ṣaḥaq,* can have sexual connotations (cf. Gen. 26:8; 39:14, 17). In some of the Canaanite cults, sacrifices were accompanied by sexual activity that was thought to induce fertility in crops, domestic animals, and humans. In the narrative, the offense stems not so much from the licentious behavior itself as from the religious apostasy that the behavior entails.

32:7-14 At first sight, it seems that Moses succeeds in softening the resolve of a God who is easily influenced by argument. In fact, like many dialogues between individuals and God recorded in the Old Testament, the conversation is part of Moses' exploration of Yahweh's true character. At first he sees the anger of God at the people's behavior. Then he recollects that Yahweh has only just liberated this very people and that he must have done this for some purpose. Is Yahweh really going to destroy them? What would the Egyptians, and especially Pharaoh, make of it? Would they not think that Yahweh was incapable of preserving his own people? What has happened to the solemn promise, that he would protect his people and get them safely through to the land he has promised them? This dialogue leads Moses to realize that *God will not destroy what he has saved.* So Yahweh "repents" (v. 14), that is, allows himself a change of heart and relents.

32:15-20   Moses climbs down the mountain. When he and Joshua hear the noise from the camp, Joshua thinks the noise is a war cry but Moses rightly discerns that it is the sound of revelry. They then find a loud orgy under way. This calls for drastic action. The covenant, like the tablets that represent it, lies in pieces at the foot of the mountain.

Moses grinds the golden bull to powder, scatters the powder on water, and orders the Israelites to drink the mixture. In Num. 5:23-28 this sort of punishment is prescribed as a test for sexual unfaithfulness. Here, below the mountain, it is a test of unfaithfulness to Yahweh. It is followed by a plague. From the biblical perspective, plague, of all the different kinds of disasters that can befall people, is a punishment inflicted by God alone (see 2 Sam. 24:14). There is an ancient Near Eastern parallel in a Ugaritic text where the god Anat slays the dragon of chaos, Mot, and then burns Mot's carcass, grinds it to pieces, and scatters it over the field. The Hebrews have been unfaithful. The substitute god has to be destroyed, and draconian measures have to be adopted so that faith may be reborn.

32:21-24   Aaron, the traditional progenitor of the priestly clan, is left standing sheepishly in the wreckage of his new religion. His excuses are comical, just like those of Adam and Eve in Genesis 2. The same syndrome of evasion and blame begun in Eden repeats itself. Aaron first blames the people ("they are bent on evil"), then implies that it was all Moses' fault for disappearing when he was most needed, then blames the fire, which somehow has managed all by itself to produce a young bull ("and there came out this calf" — by its own unaided efforts!). The contrast between the two brothers is marked. "Aaron was too weak to restrain the people; Moses was strong enough to restrain even God" (Childs, *Exodus,* 570). Moses emerges as a noble figure who not only stands physically between Israel and her deserts, but interprets Yahweh to his people as the God who saves.

32:25-29   The people's sin requires a blood sacrifice, this time for reconciliation and for propitiation. The tribe of Levi, remaining fiercely loyal to Yahweh, performs the sacrificial task by slaying the unfaithful on orders from Moses. Sacrifice, particularly atonement sacrifice, travels a long road in biblical theology. It begins with the attempted sacrifice of Isaac. It continues with the sacrifice of the firstborn in Egypt as the offering exacted from Pharaoh and the Egyptian gods for their defiance of Yahweh. It then recurs for the chosen people themselves. Here the priestly clan sheds Hebrew blood to atone for the appalling sin of the golden calf. The Day of Atonement then gathers up all offering of sacrifice for sin in one day's ritual every year. Finally, the Servant offers himself for sin (Isa. 53:10) and looks forward to the final human sacrifice of atonement, the Son of God himself.

32:30-35   Moses pleads with Yahweh to forgive the people or else blot his name from the community register kept by God (cf. Ps. 69:28; Ezek. 13:9). Yahweh insists that he will blot out the names of the transgressors. He commands Moses to lead the people to the Promised Land. Despite a hint that he will postpone definitive punishment (v. 34), the Lord sends a plague. The plague, though, is not meant to annihilate the Hebrews but to preserve a remnant. God will always preserve something of his people so that his promises will always be fulfilled.

33:1-3   Significantly, Yahweh's angel or messenger or representative accompanies them into the Promised Land at this point. Although this is an indication of God's presence, he is, because of their rebellion, not among them as he had been.

33:4-6   There is as always a need to express repentance outwardly, so the Hebrews strip off their ornaments just as they had previously surrendered their gold for the golden calf.

33:7-11 Moses, and to a lesser extent Joshua, emerges from this episode with the stature of a real mediator between Yahweh and his people. They remain at a distance, while Moses is spoken to by Yahweh "face to face, as a man speaks to his friend."

33:12-16 Moses again intercedes on the people's behalf, insisting that he and the Hebrews are utterly dependent upon their God and that he must accompany them.

33:17-23 As with the first giving of the Torah, a revelation of God precedes and authenticates the renewing of the covenant. This time Moses takes the initiative and asks to experience Yahweh's *glory,* the full weight of his *presence.* Significantly, Yahweh responds by promising a vision of his *goodness.* His overpowering glory is more than Moses can stand. So, instead of confronting God, Moses must stand in a sheltered place and be covered by Yahweh's "hand" until the glory has passed. Then he may look at Yahweh's "back." As the "holy danger" recedes, Moses can glimpse "all those qualities which call forth worship and praise" (G. B. Caird, *The Language and Imagery of the Bible,* 76).

Human imagery applied to God abounds in this passage. The anthropomorphisms are not intended to demote God but to express the reality of his personhood. Yahweh is "I"; he is the person upon whom all personhood depends, whether male or female. His statement of resolve, "I will be gracious to whom I will be gracious," is the functional equivalent to "I am who I am" (Exod. 3:14).

34:1-35 Israel has lapsed disastrously. The people's relationship with God the Creator has been utterly distorted by their worshipping him under the image of the young bull. It is now clear to Moses and to the Hebrews how God must *not* be worshipped and how the relationship with him must *not* be expressed. What follows in this chapter is not simply a parallel account of the giving of the Torah, taken from another ancient written or oral source (though from a critical study this may be so). Whoever produced the final version of the Pentateuch made a decisive theological statement in this chapter. God's forgiveness is possible and, once given, absolute. Israel must now begin again. It is also a renewed challenge to Israel *after* the incident of the golden calf. Having learned that they must not make gods out of their own resources, they must now put their trust in the *one* God and worship him alone. Far from being a tedious repetition or doublet of the traditions assembled in chapters 20–23, chapter 34 is a message for all times and places. Whenever political idols (fascist, Marxist, racist, nationalist, sectarian) crumble, whenever believers realize the selfishness or idolatry of their own lives, then the covenant with God must be renewed.

34:1-5   The renewing of the Sinai covenant begins just as impressively as the first presentation did, with a theophany of the sheer majesty of Yahweh. The radiance of the cloud appears. Moses prepares the tablets or slates, climbs the mountain, and utters the divine name. He has not been contaminated by the worship of the golden calf. Much later Moses and Elijah — those two human beings who "saw" God, communicated with him in prayer, and remained untainted by the debased religion around them — are given the privilege of flanking the Son of God and of conversing with him on the Mount of Transfiguration (Mark 9:2-8).

34:6-7   In contrast to his stern reprisal for the golden calf, Yahweh begins with a beautiful revelation of his faithfulness, since Moses and the Hebrews are now in a fit state to receive it. The "name," or character, of God is expanded into a list of qualities mostly associated with forgiveness. Yahweh is full of tenderness and empathy. He feels for and with his people. He is patient, slow to get angry. He gives out immense *hesed* love that never diminishes, and he is utterly trustworthy. He is faithful, true, reliable. This is his goodness, later to be expanded by Jesus into the beatitudes (Matthew 5) and extended to the disciples. Yahweh is not indulgent or weakly tolerant, as the punishment after the idolatry of the golden calf has shown. Thus in v. 7 we meet once again with the troubling statement that the Lord holds future generations accountable for the sins of their forebears. This statement should not be taken literally. Rather, it is intended to be a strong statement of God's justice: he does not let sin go unpunished.

34:8-17 The renewal of the covenant involves renewing the promise of the land. Once the Hebrews enter Canaan, they are to enforce what looks, at first glance, like a rigorous policy of apartheid (even ethnic cleansing). They are to engage in no offensive or defensive alliances with the present inhabitants, no "interfaith worship," no mixed marriages, and no use of existing places of worship. They are to drive out the present inhabitants of the land and eradicate all other religions. This policy was later pursued sporadically by those kings who are most praised in 1 and 2 Kings (notably, Hezekiah and Josiah) and ruthlessly imposed by Nehemiah and Ezra when Israel returned from exile in the fifth century. This passage poses immense theological and ethical problems.

First, if all the existing inhabitants of Canaan are to be driven out, why should the Hebrews need warning against dealing with them?

Second, this policy of rigid segregation falls foul of the theology of the creation stories, which show that God creates *all* human beings, male and female of every race (Gen. 1:27). It also contradicts the promise made to Abraham, and repeated three times, that he and his descendants would be a blessing to *all* the families of the earth (Gen. 12:3; 18:18; 22:18).

Third, the smashing of sacred objects and places of worship occurs again and again in human history. The Byzantine emperor, Leo, broke the icons in the twelfth century, and Cromwell's soldiers defaced many an English church and cathedral in the seventeenth century. This sort of action is now rightly considered to be brutally intolerant, a form of self-defeating vandalism. At the very least, it is the wrong way of going about evangelism. At best, it ill accords with the loving concern for all peoples shown in various places in the Old Testament, such as in the book of Jonah, and in the behavior of Jesus himself.

Fourth, apartheid, or racism (by no means restricted to South Africa), appears to be justified on religious grounds here. If people hold a religious point of view strongly enough and believe in racial exclusivism passionately enough, then they are obliged to exterminate or at least convert all those who do not agree.

The context is vital to a proper understanding of the biblical perspective on intolerance toward the inhabitants of Canaan. The Hebrews have just worshipped the golden calf. The solemn bond between Israel and Yahweh has been ruptured and must be reestablished in the clearest possible terms. In the ancient world, alliances with other peoples were not only alliances with humans but with their gods as well. If the Hebrews were to enter into such alliances, it would lead to more golden calves (Solomon provides an example from later Israelite history). Mixed marriages would similarly lead to apostasy (again, look at Solomon). A place of worship in working order would constitute an open invitation to worship the deity of that shrine, if only to see if that other god proved to be more liberal or amenable. These are the perceptions that stand behind the stark warnings to a people who proved themselves only too prone to forget the God to whom they were bound. This is the paradox that Jews and Christians (and, indeed, Muslims) have to face. Put in Christians terms, Jesus died and rose from the dead for *all* people, many of whom show no inclination, or have no realistic opportunity, to worship him or become his disciples. This is the dilemma of interfaith relationships — the unique nature of our faith and the acceptance of others together with their beliefs and practices.

34:18-26   The instructions that follow were carefully chosen to act as reminders and warnings to the Hebrews. The feast of Unleavened Bread, because of its linking with Passover, is to be kept as a strong reminder that Yahweh has liberated them from Egypt. Similarly, the rules for firstborn sacrifices remind the people of the last plague, the sacrifice of the Egyptian firstborn. The Sabbath is to be carefully observed as a reminder that Yahweh is both Creator and Liberator.

Next, instructions are given concerning two pilgrim or trek feasts, for which everyone, or at least all males, must travel to one designated place. The first *ḥag* is the feast of Weeks, so called because it was observed seven weeks after Passover. This festival came at the end of the grape harvest, the last ingathering of the year, and celebrated the gift of the Promised Land to the Hebrews. They would be so secure in that land that the men could all go away from home for the feast, leaving the women and children, the aged, and the infirm at home. The Passover is also described here as a *ḥag*, though it was originally celebrated in the family setting, at home. Outside Exodus 12, there are few references to Passover in the Old Testament. Its revival is linked with Josiah's reforms (2 Kgs. 23:21-23), and it must have gained increasing significance during and after the Exile. Certainly, by Jesus' time Passover had acquired a whole wealth of meaning, so that he deliberately chose that feast for his death and resurrection.

34:27-35 Moses' previous descent from the mountain had been in anger, to confront the mischief of the golden calf. This time he comes down in glory. His face shines with rays of light emanating from his very person. (Several painters and sculptors over the centuries have illustrated Moses with two horns projecting from his head. This arose from a mistranslation of the original Hebrew verb "to shine," which resembles the word for "horn" — an unfortunate and misleading error). The implications of the light shining from Moses are immense. Moses is a human being; no claim is made for him being anything more than human. Yet he is permitted to share in the glory that belongs to God. God has created everything, yet he chooses to share his godhead in some measure with a fallible human being, so fallible that Moses is subsequently not allowed into the Promised Land. When the people see this, they are in awe of Moses and also take it as a visible sign of their forgiveness. The Christian churches in the West, unlike their counterparts in the East, have made all too little of the Transfiguration of Jesus (Mark 9:2-8). There, three human beings, two of them long since dead, were seen conversing together as human beings converse with each other, yet surrounded by divine glory. The message is that human beings are created for glory, the glory shared with them by their loving Creator. This visible sign of God's glory shared with human beings has not been restricted to Jesus and his two Old Testament companions. To take but one example, in nineteenth-century

Russia a disciple of Seraphim of Sarov, a solitary monk who went and lived out in the Siberian steppe, was challenged by Seraphim to look at him. The disciple replied. "I cannot look at you, father, because lightning flashes from your eyes. Your face has become brighter than the sun, and my eyes ache."

In order to calm the people's fear, Moses puts a covering (possibly a mask) over his face. Paul pointed out that, if the revelation of the Torah caused Moses' face to shine, how much greater would be the glory shining from the very person of God as revealed in Jesus Christ (2 Cor. 3:7-18). He could have added that the revolutionary message that God will share his own glory with a mere human being was extended in Jesus to humanity as a whole.

GOD'S FORGIVEN PEOPLE
Exodus 35:1–40:38

These chapters are usually ascribed by scholars to the Priestly writer of the exile in Babylon. This sensible conjecture should not prejudice our understanding of them. These chapters record how the instructions given to Moses for building the tabernacle were carried out. These chapters repeat much of what is in chapters 25 to 31, with some variation in order, but they are not careless, random repetitions.

The golden calf has been made — and destroyed. The Hebrews have come perilously near to all-out rebellion against Yahweh and have rejected him. Yet he has not given up on them. Because his patience and love are endless, he is prepared to begin again. So the covenant is renewed, the tabernacle is constructed, and the system of worship is inaugurated. The people's response to the shock of betraying their God is to give as much as possible and to work as hard as possible. If sin against God provokes repentance and amendment, it is never total disaster. The Hebrews' repentance is shown in enthusiasm for the future worship of Yahweh *alone* by sacrifice in the tabernacle through a properly constituted priesthood. The final dedication of the whole is a rededication of Israel as a whole to Yahweh.

Once this is grasped, then the practical questions can be faced. For instance, could all this activity have taken place in a desert landscape? Do not the architecture of the tabernacle and the system of worship belong to a much more sophisticated setting, namely, the Jerusalem Temple? What has often escaped commentators is that the compiler of this account may well not have been unaware of the obvious discrepancies between a barren desert and what was supposed to have been done there.

The real message of these chapters is not historical accuracy or anachronism. The message of Exodus 35–40 concerns Yahweh's forgiveness and Israel's willingness to begin again. Seen against the wider canvas of biblical theology, the tabernacle and the sacrifices offered in it, in all their profusion and detail, proclaim a simple message. Human beings sin and make for themselves golden calves; yet each time they turn back to God he forgives them, and they return with enthusiasm to him, only to find that he has anticipated their need of a sacrifice and has provided one already, in the Cross.

35:1-3 All the work now in progress on the tabernacle is enclosed and sanctified by the Sabbath. The Hebrews stop work and offer the day, and the week, to the Lord. Compare 31:12-17.

35:4-19 The emphasis in this project of the tabernacle is *generosity*. There is to be no skimping in the providing of materials and skills in profusion. Yahweh has generously forgiven; the people generously respond. Compare 25:1-9.

35:20-29 It is easy to get lost in a list of materials given for this or that purpose. It is the enthusiasm and willingness of all the people that stands out. "Everyone whose heart was *stirred* . . . whose spirit was *willing* . . . brought the LORD's offering. . . . So they came, both men and women; all who were of a *willing* heart . . . ." This is a busy scene, in which the sheer pleasure of working for Yahweh comes across, together with a sense of selflessness and happiness. Verse 29 sums it all up in the words "freewill offering." This is not an unwilling people being forced to give up their precious time and few possessions, but a grateful people giving without grudging to their great and loving God.

35:30–36:3 Two master craftsmen are specifically named, Bezalel and Oholiab. These men are "filled with divine spirit, with skill, intelligence, and knowledge in every kind of craft." They have manual and logistic skills, *given by God*. It is well worth noting that no distinction is made here between spiritual, intellectual gifts of the Spirit and physical gifts. The former are not

141

"higher"; the latter are not "lower." The Spirit of God comes upon his servants and empowers them for the work. A contrast is sometimes made between the way the Spirit comes upon isolated individuals, like Bezalel and the prophets, in the Old Testament, and the way the Spirit comes upon the whole Church in the New Testament. The Bible, however, never makes this contrast. In both the Old and New Testaments, certain people are endowed with certain gifts for certain purposes, with no guarantee that these gifts are gifts for life. Both testaments, however, also emphasize the corporate nature of the people of God, whether Israel or the Christian Church. The famous promise in the book of Joel (2:28-29) is addressed to Israel as a whole and looks forward to the empowering of *all flesh* (the whole of humanity) with the Spirit. When Paul emphasizes that the gifts of the Spirit, though given through individuals, are for the building up of the *whole* community (1 Corinthians 12), he is applying the theology of these verses of Exodus to the Christian Church. Bezalel and Oholiab are not solo artists, but charismatic servants of Yahweh and of the community.

36:4-7   The Hebrews give so enthusiastically that Moses has to call a halt to the gifts and offers of labor. This is how the response to God's generosity should be.

36:8-38   The service of Yahweh deserves only and always the *best*, the very best, expressed in beauty and craftsmanship. Compare 26:1-37.

37:1-38:8   In this account Bezalel, the gifted engineer and architect, is responsible for all the work — the ark (37:1-9; cf. 25:10-22), the table and vessels (37:10-16; cf. 25:23-30), the "altar" of incense (37:25-28; cf. 30:1-10), as well as the hollow altar of sacrifice and the basin for ablutions (38:1-8; cf. 27:1-8). Bezalel must have left a tremendous reputation behind him as a Leonardo da Vinci of the Hebrews. Because he was specifically endowed with the Spirit, the tabernacle sanctuary — like its successor, the Jerusalem Temple — becomes the direct design of Yahweh himself. God gives the skills; the people give the materials and the labor. Thus inspiration, hard work, and faith unite in giving abiding identity to the people of God.

38:9-20   These verses describe the construction of the outer area, and this time Bezalel, is only mentioned once, at the beginning. Compare 27:9-19.

38:21-23   The three leading personalities, Ithamar, Bezalel, and Oholiab, are given special mention. Just as the tabernacle reflects creation, so also do these three humans, empowered by God's Spirit, become partners with God in creating Israel's system of worship.

38:24-31   To us, who live some three thousand years later, the quantity surveyor's analysis may seem irrelevant. The meaning of it all is *not* irrelevant, though. Yahweh the Creator and Rescuer must be served with attention to every exact detail. The measurements are not intended to record a historical inventory, but to give a message to succeeding generations. "Put all your energy and skills at the service of your God at all times."

39:1-31   The vestments are listed in a riot of colorful and enthusiastic detail. First comes the ephod, then the twelve semi-precious stones, "according to the names of the sons of Israel." Then follows the mantle with its fringe of interspersed golden balls and pomegranates, and the tunics. Last comes the medallion, inscribed "Holy to the Lord," for the high priest's turban. Those words sum up the tabernacle and, indeed, the whole people of Israel. Compare 28:1-43.

39:32-43   Moses inspects the completed work, is satisfied, and blesses the workers. These verses seem to reflect a combination of separate traditions concerning the tent and the tabernacle, to which we may compare 26:7-14.

40:1-33   The dedication of the whole shrine is appointed for the first day of the first month. This is an obvious reference both to the creation (Genesis 1) and to the Sabbath. The dedication constitutes an act of creation, of forming God's people, and of setting apart the whole (creation, Israel, worship, the tabernacle) to the Lord.

The tabernacle is assembled (vv. 1-8) and anointed with oil (vv. 9-11). The priests wash themselves and are consecrated. Aaron is vested and anointed (v. 13) and his sons too (vv. 14-15). They will form the perpetual, hereditary priesthood. The tabernacle is then finally erected. Compare 30:26-30.

The whole relationship between the Hebrews and Yahweh is thus expressed in a detailed and permanent way. The message is not, "This is exactly what was done and enacted at a certain date and in a certain place, with a modern historian's accuracy." Rather, the message is, "I am your God and I will be with you always. You will relate to me in the careful offering of sacrifice at a specific holy place set apart for worship of me *alone*."

Worship is the meeting of the natural with the supernatural, of the creation with its Creator, of people with God. It is the most important task that people can undertake. It is the visible sign of faithfulness to God. This perspective explains the extensive space given to liturgical instructions in Scripture, from Exodus's description of the tabernacle, to Ezekiel's design for the new temple, to Paul's very different but equally explicit instructions to the Corinthians, to the book of Revelation's vision of worship in heaven.

40:37-38 The journey is resumed. Yahweh again accompanies his people in the pillar of cloud and fire. But they must strike camp and pitch camp at *his* commands. When the cloud moves, they plod on. When it halts, they halt. At Yahweh's pace, his people move toward the Promised Land.

SELECTED BIBLIOGRAPHY

Ashby, Godfrey W. *Sacrifice: Its Nature and Purpose.* London: SCM, 1988.

Brooks, Roger. *The Spirit of the Ten Commandments: Shattering the Myth of Rabbinic Legalism.* San Francisco: Harper & Row, 1990.

Caird, G. B. *The Language and Imagery of the Bible.* London: Duckworth; Philadelphia: Westminster, 1980. Reprint, Grand Rapids: Eerdmans, 1997.

Childs, Brevard S. *The Book of Exodus: A Critical, Theological Commentary.* Old Testament Library. London: SCM, 1974.

Cole, Robert Alan. *Exodus.* Tyndale Old Testament Commentaries. Downers Grove, IL: Inter-Varsity, 1973.

Craigie, Peter C. *Ugarit and the Old Testament.* Grand Rapids: Eerdmans, 1983.

Croatto, J. Severino. *Exodus: A Hermeneutics of Freedom.* Rev. ed. Maryknoll, NY: Orbis, 1981.

Davies, Gordon F. *Israel in Egypt: Reading Exodus 1–2.* JSOT Supplement Series 135. Sheffield: JSOT Press, 1992.

Fretheim, Terence E. *Exodus.* Interpretation: A Commentary for Teaching and Preaching. Louisville: John Knox, 1991.

Gowan, Donald E. *Theology in Exodus: Biblical Theology in the Form of a Commentary.* Louisville: Westminster John Knox, 1994.

Greenberg, Moshe. *Understanding Exodus.* New York: Behrman, 1969.

Guttierrez, Gustavo. *A Theology of Liberation: History, Politics, and Salvation.* Maryknoll, NY: Orbis, 1973.

Harrelson, Walter. *The Ten Commandments and Human Rights.* Philadelphia: Fortress, 1980.

Hyatt, J. Philip. *Exodus.* The New Century Bible Commentary. Grand Rapids: Eerdmans, 1980.

145

Knight, George A. F. *Theology as Narration: A Commentary on the Book of Exodus*. Grand Rapids: Eerdmans, 1976.

Levenson, Jon, *Sinai and Zion: An Entry into the Jewish Bible*. Minneapolis: Winston, 1985.

Mendenhall, George E. *Law and Covenant in Israel and the Ancient Near East*. Pittsburgh: Biblical Colloquium, 1955.

Nicholson, Ernest W. *God and His People: Covenant and Theology in the Old Testament*. Oxford: Clarendon, 1986.

Noth, Martin, *Exodus*. Old Testament Library. Philadelphia: Westminster, 1962.

Phillips, Anthony. *Ancient Israel's Criminal Law*. Oxford: Blackwell, 1970.

Pritchard, James B., ed. *Ancient Near Eastern Texts Relating to the Old Testament*. Third Edition with Supplement. Princeton: Princeton University Press, 1969.

Rad, Gerhard von. *Holy War in Ancient Israel*. Translated and edited by Marva J. Dawn. Introduction by Ben C. Ollenburger. Bibliography by Judith E. Sanderson. Grand Rapids: Eerdmans, 1991.

———— *Old Testament Theology*. 2 vols. Edinburgh: Oliver & Boyd; New York: Harper & Row, 1962-65.

Rendtorff, Rolf. *Canon and Theology: Overtures to an Old Testament Theology*. Overtures to Biblical Theology. Minneapolis: Fortress, 1993.

Sarna, Nahum M. *Exodus*. The JPS Torah Commentary. Philadelphia: The Jewish Publication Society, 1991.

Segal, J. Ben-Zion, ed. *The Ten Commandments in History and Tradition*. Jerusalem: Magnes, 1990.

de Vaux, Roland, *Ancient Israel: Its Life and Institutions*. London: Darton, Longman & Todd, 1961. Reprint, Grand Rapids: Eerdmans, 1997.

———— *Studies in Old Testament Sacrifice*. Cardiff: University of Wales Press, 1964.

Whybray, R. Norman. *Introduction to the Pentateuch*. Grand Rapids: Eerdmans, 1995.